English
Cottage Quilts

English Cottage

Quilts

10 Charming Projects

PAMELA MOSTEK

Martingale®
& COMPANY

Dedication

To the Greens—Michael, Maggie, Toby, and Belinda—our family in England,
who introduced me to the captivating charm of the English countryside.

English Cottage Quilts:
10 Charming Projects
© 2004 by Pamela Mostek

Martingale®
& COMPANY

That Patchwork Place®

That Patchwork Place® is an imprint
of Martingale & Company®.

Martingale & Company
20205 144th Avenue NE
Woodinville, WA 98072-8478
www.martingale-pub.com

Credits

President: Nancy J. Martin
CEO: Daniel J. Martin
Publisher: Jane Hamada
Editorial Director: Mary V. Green
Managing Editor: Tina Cook
Technical Editor: Laurie Baker
Copy Editor: Liz McGehee
Design Director: Stan Green
Illustrator: Laurel Strand
Location Photographer: Toby Green
Studio Photographer: Brent Kane
Cover and Text Designer: Stan Green

Mission Statement

Dedicated to providing quality products
and service to inspire creativity.

Printed in China
09 08 07 06 05 04   8 7 6 5 4 3 2 1

Library of Congress Cataloging-in-Publication Data

Mostek, Pamela.
    English cottage quilts / Pamela Mostek.
        p. cm.
    ISBN 1-56477-475-9
    1. Patchwork—Patterns. 2. Quilting—Patterns.
3. Cottages in art. I. Title.
    TT835.M692 2004
    746.46'041—dc22
                                                    2003016706

Acknowledgments

Putting this book together was a true labor of love—and a true challenge! Coordinating and planning between my home in Washington State and the home of *English Cottage Quilts* in Nayland, United Kingdom, took the help and assistance of many people. I couldn't have pulled it all together without them. Here are a few that deserve a special thank-you:

To Martingale & Company, once again, for having faith in my vision of a beautiful and unique book. I appreciate the wonderful opportunity to make that vision come true.

To Toby Green, my fantastic photographer, for sharing my enthusiasm for the book and for all the extra effort and energy he put into the whole project.

To my husband, Bob, for his unyielding confidence in my abilities and ideas. And for his help and support when it came to hauling trunks of precious quilts to the other side of the world to photograph. He made a terrific photographer's assistant, too!

To Maggie Green, my friend and sister-in-law in Nayland, who helped me round up props, find shooting locations, and generally lent her knowledge of the village and her moral support to the whole project.

To Michael Green, my brother-in-law, for being such a great "front man" and helping with the advance details. As he said, maybe I was a proper English girl in another life!

To the folks in Nayland, who were hospitable and patient while we photographed the quilts. I hope they will enjoy seeing their charming village in this book!

To Carol MacQuarrie, my friend and quilter, who takes such good care of me and my quilts! I couldn't get it all done without her help putting my projects at the top of the list and handling each of them with such loving care.

To Edi Dobbins, my friend and seamstress, who rescues me periodically with her expert piecing and great advice. Thanks to her for finding some of those little details that need to be worked out.

To my daughters, Stacey and Rachel, who have always been my inspiration for being a hard-working, highly motivated, mountain-moving mom!

And to my precious grandchildren, Jared, Lauren, Josie, and Brooke, who bring joy and smiles to any day and always remind me what is really important.

A special thanks to the following companies that generously provided materials or tools for this book:

Marcus Brothers Textiles, Inc.; In The Beginning Fabrics; Erlanger Group, Ltd.; Robert Kaufman Co., Inc.; and Starr Designs, for the gorgeous fabrics that I used in the quilts.

Air-Lite Synthetic Manufacturing, Inc., for their wonderful cotton batting, which creates the traditional flat-quilted look that I prefer.

Creative Grids, for introducing me to their wonderful see-through rulers with gripping dots on the back. They made my life much easier!

Pfaff sales and marketing, for supplying the amazing Pfaff creative 2140, which I used to sew the quilts in this book.

Contents

An English Cottage Welcome

Storybook cottages in sherbet colors of peach, pink, yellow, and green, and a narrow cobblestone street that winds among them—this was my first sight of the English village of Nayland. Here I was, an eager American on my first visit to the English countryside, and I was captivated.

It was like no other place I had seen, this picturesque village that seemed like a step back in history. There were ancient stone walls, a village churchyard with centuries-old gravestones, and enchanted gardens that took my breath away, especially when I realized that most were centuries older than our whole country!

Then there were the gardens. Now, I admit to being easily impressed by gorgeous gardens. There's nothing I love more than the flash of color and tangle of blooms in a cottage-style garden. But these gardens were unique. Rambling red and yellow roses bloomed profusely, covering the sides of cottages and surrounding doorways. Tall stalks of hollyhocks popped through the cracks in the walkways, blooming just about

anywhere. And the huge, abundant vines that covered everything—I fantasized that they must be centuries old!

Since that magical first visit, I have returned a number of times. Each time I am once again captivated . . . and that is how this book began. I am a quilt designer, and to me, a lovely location is the perfect inspiration for creating memorable quilts. In my walks through the village, I envisioned a lovely quilt spread in the garden for reading or draped on a table set with English china and ready for afternoon tea. The ideas were endless, and I was ready to begin.

Creating the quilts and making plans to present them in this book was a labor of love. I hope you will be pleased with the results. And visiting the village once

again to photograph the quilts was a great adventure! I held my breath that everything would arrive on time and undamaged—and it did! My thanks go out to all the local folks who were so kind and hospitable to us as we set up our shots and took the photos.

I've tried to capture my affection for the look, feel, and historical charm of an English village, which is very far from my busy life in the United States but very close to my heart. I hope, too, that you may decide to create a quilt that is inspired by a favorite spot in your own life—a trip to majestic mountains, a brilliant sunset over an ocean beach, or even the garden view from your own back door. Anything that you treasure is the perfect start for a quilt that is uniquely your own.

Enjoy your visit to the village of Nayland as you browse through the pages of this book—and have fun creating the quilts that this storybook spot inspired.

Pam

About Nayland

When Columbus visited America in the 1400s, many of the homes in this village were already standing. In fact, some had been here for centuries, as the history of Nayland dates back to medieval times. A country village in the classic English style, it is located in the Suffolk region, about an hour northeast of London. Nestled in the midst of farmland and rolling hills, it joins many other villages in the area in offering visitors an enchanting look at the English countryside of storybook tales.

A Walk through the Village

As I strolled through the village streets of Nayland,

I was struck by the feeling that time had stood still in this quaint spot.

I had visited the busy and bustling city of London, but this was a totally different world.

Everywhere I looked were reminders of the centuries-old roots of this part of the world. The plastered homes painted in pastel shades were supported by ancient timbers that were anything but straight. In fact, because of these primitive and oftentimes crooked timbers, some houses themselves appeared to be standing at an angle! Of course, I could just see a quilt in shades of green and cream hanging from the upstairs window of one of those peach or pink houses! "Cobblestones" on page 98 is the result of that vision!

The houses are very close to the street, and at first I didn't see a garden anywhere. But the surprise was in the back! Tucked away behind the homes are the lovely cottage gardens that inspired "Maggie's Garden" (page 34) and "Chain of Ivy" (page 42).

Then there was the amazing fireplace in the dining room of one of the village homes, Noll Gate House. We could actually sit inside the fireplace, which is believed to have been constructed in the fourteenth century. Naturally I envisioned a table set with English china

With lovely, abundant gardens along its bank, an idyllic stream winds its way through the village. Here you see a charming summer house nestled among the blooms—a perfect spot for enjoying tea and the beauty of the greenery on a summer afternoon.

and a classic-looking quilt. This was the inspiration for "China Blue" (page 76), which was photographed ready for a cozy meal in front of the fireplace.

I've also included some tips and other quick ideas to go along with your quilted projects. Accompanying "Lavender Tea" (page 68), you'll find a delightful recipe to serve at afternoon tea, and you'll learn about Open Gardens, the popular open house held in the village gardens to raise money each summer for charity. Perhaps it would be a great event to start in your own community!

England has its own quilting heritage. A lovely example is Durham quilting, the elegant style of hand quilting used on what we would today call whole-cloth quilts. You'll find out a little more about this craft's history and how to adapt it to today's machine-quilting techniques.

Your tour of the village will continue as you travel through the pages of this book. Each project was beautifully photographed in the spot that inspired it and is often accompanied by information about the village.

So, with this brief introduction, you're ready to begin exploring the village. I hope you'll enjoy your visit and the wonderful quilts you'll find along the way.

Welcoming spring, brilliant red poppies and wildflowers burst into bloom in the fields that surround the village.

Chintz Bouquets

$\mathcal{C}$harming chintz florals—nothing evokes vintage English style

like a collection of these traditional prints in a variety of garden colors.

In this quilt, these dainty classics have come together in basket bouquets of appliquéd

flowers. How appropriate for them to be adorning the front of Alston Court,

one of the oldest and finest medieval townhouses in Britain.

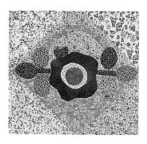

Materials

Yardage is based on 42"-wide fabric.

- 2⅛ yards total of assorted chintz prints for block backgrounds
- 1⅝ yards of pink chintz print for border and binding
- 1½ yards of tan chintz print for baskets
- ½ yard of green chintz print for narrow border and vines
- ⅜ yard of rose chintz print for narrow border
- Assorted scraps of rose, pink, purple, yellow, and green fabrics for flower and leaf appliqués
- 3¾ yards of fabric for backing
- 65" x 65" square of batting
- ⅜" and ½" bias bars
- Fabric glue stick
- Freezer paper

Cutting

All measurements include ¼"-wide seam allowances.

From the assorted chintz prints, cut a total of:

8 squares, 8⅞" x 8⅞"; cut each square in half once diagonally to yield 16 half-square triangles

32 squares, 7" x 7"; cut each square in half once diagonally to yield 64 half-square triangles

From the tan chintz print, cut:

2 strips, 8⅞" x 42"; crosscut into 8 squares, each 8⅞" x 8⅞". Cut each square in half once diagonally to yield 16 half-square triangles.

From the green chintz print, cut:

7 strips, 1" x 42"; crosscut 1 strip into:
   1 strip, 1" x 21"
   4 rectangles, 1" x 4½"

3 strips, 1¼" x 42"; crosscut into
   16 rectangles, 1¼" x 6"

From the pink chintz print for borders and binding, cut:

7 strips, 3½" x 42"; cut 1 strip in half crosswise to yield 2 strips, 3½" x 21" (1 left over)

7 strips, 1" x 42"; cut 1 strip in half crosswise to yield 2 strips, 1" x 21" (1 left over)

7 strips, 2¾" x 42"

From the rose chintz print, cut:

7 strips, 1" x 42"; crosscut 1 strip into:
   4 rectangles, 1" x 4½"
   4 rectangles, 1" x 5½"

Chintz Bouquets

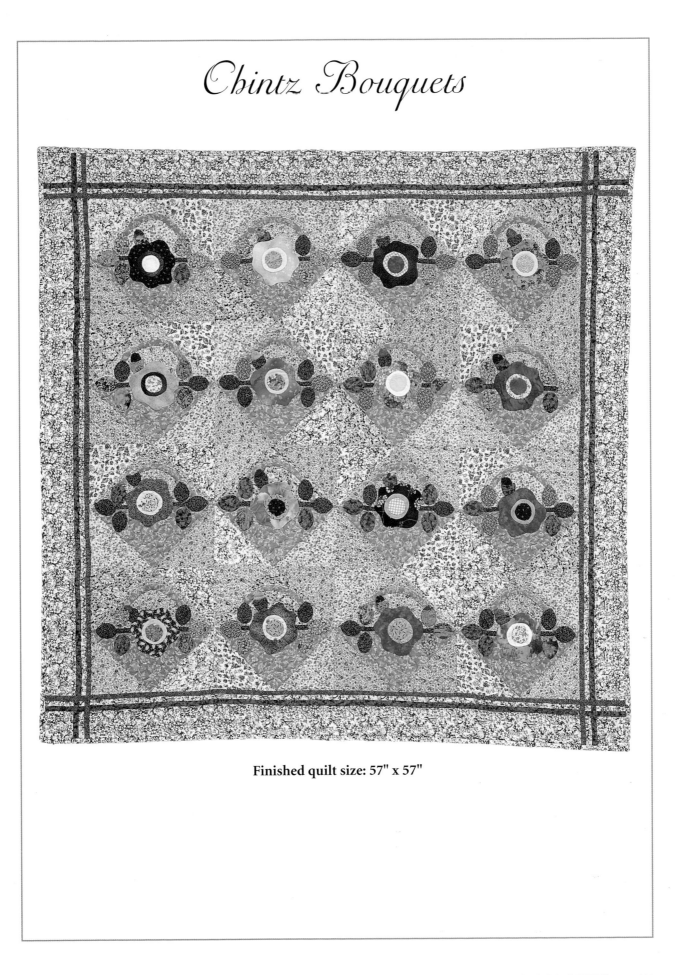

Finished quilt size: 57" x 57"

Making the Blocks

1. To make the basket handles, refer to "Cutting Bias Strips" on page 106 and cut approximately 200" of 1½"-wide bias strips from the remaining tan chintz fabric. Sew the strips together end to end to make one long strip. Using the ½" bias bar, refer to the manufacturer's instructions to stitch the bias strip into a tube. Cut the tube into 16 pieces, each 12" long.

2. Position a bias tube on each of the 16 assorted chintz 8⅞" half-square triangles as shown. Make sure that the ends of the tube extend slightly beyond the edge of the triangle so that they can be caught easily in the seam. Use the glue stick to temporarily adhere the tubes in place.

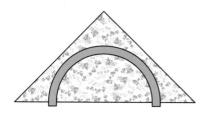

3. Position each basket handle triangle from step 2 on top of a tan chintz triangle, right sides together. Sew the triangles together along the bias edges, catching the ends of the handles in the seam. Press the seam allowances open.

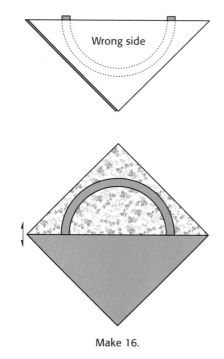

Make 16.

4. Sew an assorted chintz print 7" half-square triangle to each side of the basket units from step 3 as shown,

---

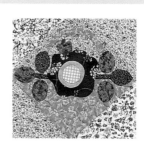

Appliqué Kits

This is a great project to do while you're on the road or away from home. I did all of the appliqué for this quilt while traveling. I prepared the appliqué pieces at one time, then placed the pieces I needed for each block, plus the block itself, into a separate plastic bag, making 16 appliqué kits! I assembled the threads and needles in another bag, and I was ready to go. Whenever I headed out the door, I grabbed an appliqué kit for a block or two and my threads. Not only did I save precious time but the miles went by quickly, too!

stitching opposite sides first. Press the seam allowances open. Stay stitch close to the edge of each block to prevent the edges from stretching during the appliqué process.

remaining shapes, working in alphabetical order. Remove the freezer paper.

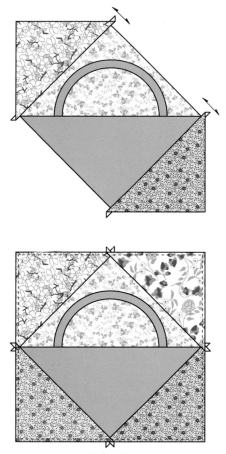

Make 16.

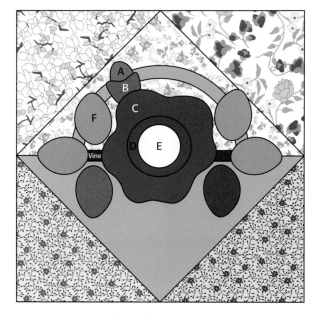

Appliqué Placement Guide

5. Using the ⅜" bias bar, stitch each green chintz 1¼" x 6" rectangle into a tube. Cut each segment in half crosswise to make 32 vine pieces that are 3" long.

6. Referring to "Freezer-Paper Appliqué" on page 105, trace the required number of patterns A–F on page 33. Adhere the freezer-paper shapes to the wrong side of the appropriate assorted chintz scraps and cut them out. Follow the appliqué placement guide to appliqué the vine pieces from step 5 in place on each Basket block from step 4. Then appliqué the

7. Square up and trim each of the appliquéd blocks so that there is a ¼" seam allowance extending beyond each of the basket points. The trimmed blocks should measure 12½" x 12½".

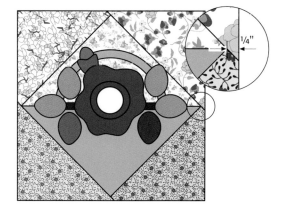

Assembling the Quilt Top

1. Referring to the quilt assembly diagram on the facing page, arrange the blocks into four rows of four blocks each, rearranging the blocks as necessary until you are pleased with the position of the chintz prints. Sew the blocks in each row together. Press the seams in alternate directions from row to row. Sew the rows together. Press the seams in one direction.

2. Sew the 3½" x 21" and 1" x 21" pink chintz strips to the 1" x 21" green chintz strip as shown to make a strip set. Press the seams toward the pink strips. Cut the strip set into four 3½"-wide segments and four 1"-wide segments.

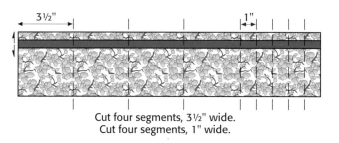

Cut four segments, 3½" wide.
Cut four segments, 1" wide.

3. Assemble the corner blocks as shown below, using the segments from step 2, the green 1" x 4½" rectangles, and the rose 1" x 4½" and 1" x 5½" rectangles. Make four blocks.

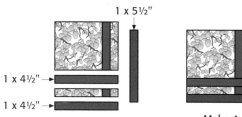

Make 4.

4. To make the borders, cut two of the six remaining 3½" x 42" pink chintz strips in half crosswise. Sew each half-length strip to the end of a full-length strip. Repeat with the 1"-wide pink, green, and rose chintz strips.

5. Stitch one pink chintz print 3½"-wide strip and one strip *each* of the 1"-wide pink chintz print, green chintz, and rose chintz together to make a strip set. Make 4. Trim each strip set to 48½".

Make 4.

6. Stitch a border strip to the quilt sides, placing the rose strip closest to the quilt top. Sew a corner block to each end of the remaining border strips, being sure to orient the blocks correctly. Stitch the strips to the top and bottom edges of the quilt top as shown.

Finishing Your Quilt

Refer to "General Instructions," beginning on page 105, for specific instructions for each of the following finishing steps.

1. Layer the quilt top with batting and backing; baste.

2. Quilt the assorted chintz triangles with heavy stipple quilting. For the basket triangles, quilt in a cross-hatch pattern to emphasize the texture of the basket. Leave the appliquéd flowers and leaves and the green and rose border strips unquilted.

3. Use the 2¾"-wide chintz strips to bind the quilt edges.

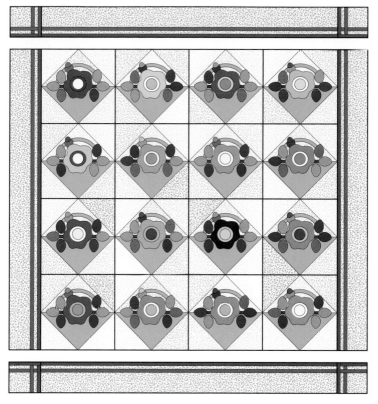

Quilt Assembly Diagram

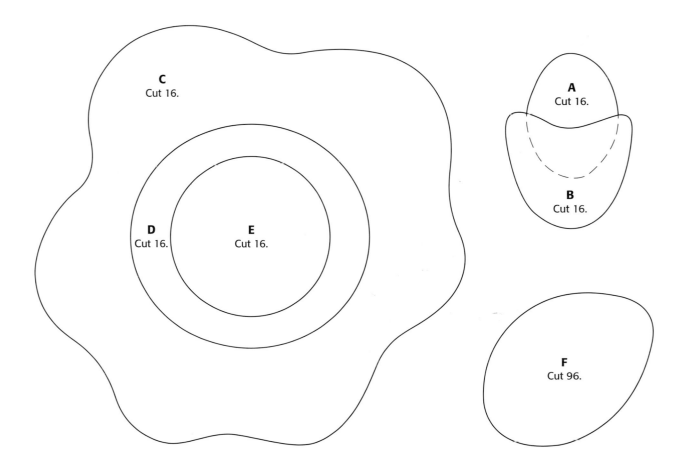

C
Cut 16.

A
Cut 16.

B
Cut 16.

D
Cut 16.

E
Cut 16.

F
Cut 96.

Maggie's Garden

$\mathcal{E}$verywhere you look, gorgeous red roses are blooming

in Maggie's English garden. Just as in the garden, roses are sprinkled

among the other lively colors of this breathtaking quilt. By fussy cutting the roses,

you can "plant" them in the blocks to create your own unique scrappy quilt.

Materials

Yardage is based on 42"-wide fabric.

- 5 yards of rose print for blocks, border, and binding*
- 2 yards of assorted light-value solids and small prints that coordinate with rose print, for blocks
- 2 yards of assorted medium- and dark-value solids and small prints that coordinate with rose print, for blocks
- 4⅛ yards of fabric for backing
- 68" x 84" piece of batting
- 4½" square clear ruler (optional)

*Additional yardage has been allowed to fussy cut the roses. You may need more or less yardage, depending on the print.

Cutting

All measurements include ¼"-wide seam allowances.

From the assorted light-value fabrics, cut a *total* of:

192 squares, 2⅞" x 2⅞"

From the assorted medium- and dark-value fabrics, cut a *total* of:

192 squares, 2⅞" x 2⅞"

From the remaining assorted light-, medium-, and dark-value fabrics, cut a *total* of:

116 squares, 2½" x 2½"

464 squares, 1½" x 1½"

From the rose print, cut:

7 strips, 6½" x 42"

7 strips, 2¾" x 42"

38 squares, 4½" x 4½", each centered on a rose

Fussy Cutting

The squares from the rose print should all be fussy cut. Fussy cutting is the technique of cutting out a specific part of the print fabric to use in a design. The best way to cut out these squares is to use a see-through ruler that is the same size as the block you will be using. Position the ruler on the fabric where you want to cut a flower, remembering that ¼" on each side will be hidden in the seam allowance. Then cut out the square.

Maggie's Garden

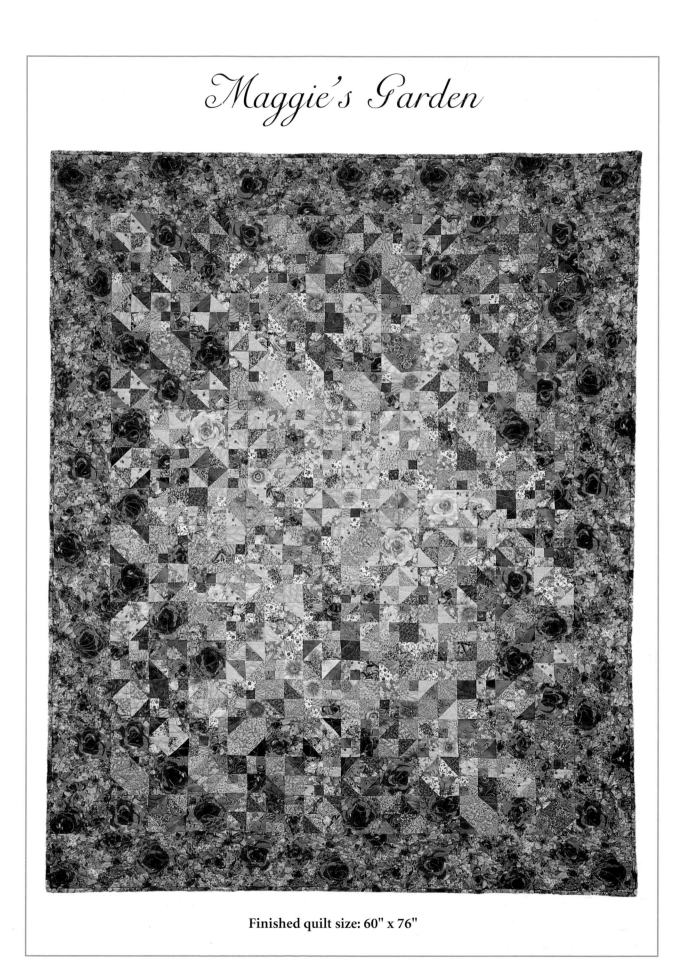

Finished quilt size: 60" x 76"

Making the Blocks

1. **To make block A,** use a soft-lead pencil to draw a diagonal line from corner to corner on the wrong side of 76 assorted light-value 2⅞" squares. Place each square right sides together with an assorted medium- or dark-value 2⅞" square. Using your presser foot as a guide, stitch ¼" from each side of the diagonal line on each square. Cut along the drawn lines with a scissors to make a total of 152 half-square triangles. Press the seams toward the darker triangles.

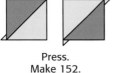

Stitch.　　　Cut.

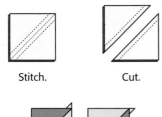

Press.
Make 152.

2. Group the half-square triangles from step 1 into like pairs. Arrange and sew two sets of pairs together as shown. Repeat to make a total of 38 half-square-triangle units.

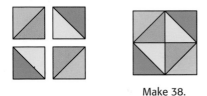

Make 38.

3. Sew 304 assorted-value 1½" squares together in pairs. Sew the pairs of squares together as shown to make 76 four-patch squares.

Make 76.

4. Sew two four-patch squares from step 3 together with two assorted-value 2½" squares as shown. Repeat to make a total of 38 four-patch units.

Make 38.

5. Sew two half-square-triangle units from step 2 and two four-patch units from step 4 together as shown to make block A. The block should measure 8½" x 8½". Repeat to make a total of 19 block A.

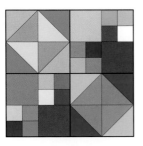

Block A
Make 19.

Piecing the Blocks

Have fun putting together your scrappy blocks. The three block variations are like miniquilts because you have fabric choices for each block. To give your quilt that added sparkle and contrast, create a variety of values in your blocks. For some, use all darker fabrics; for others, use all lighter choices. For still others, mix up the values. I made about six to eight of mine with lots of yellow fabrics and placed them near the center of the quilt. It may help to refer to the quilt assembly diagram on page 40 before you begin making the blocks so you can plan fabric placement.

6. **To make block B,** repeat steps 1 and 2, pairing 80 assorted light-value 2⅞" squares with 80 assorted medium or dark-value 2⅞" squares. Cut the squares apart and sew two sets of pairs together to make 40 half-square-triangle units.

7. Using 40 assorted-value 2½" squares and 160 assorted-value 1½" squares, repeat steps 3 and 4 of block A to make 20 four-patch units.

8. Sew two half-square-triangle units, one four-patch unit, and one rose-print square together as shown to make block B. The block should measure 8½" x 8½". Repeat to make a total of 20 block B.

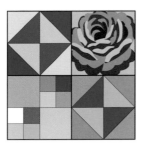

Block B
Make 20.

9. **To make block C,** repeat steps 1 and 2, pairing 36 light-value 2⅞" squares with 36 medium- or dark-value 2⅞" squares. Cut the squares apart and sew two sets of pairs together to make 18 half-square-triangle units.

10. Sew two half-square-triangle units and two rose-print squares together as shown to make block C. The block should measure 8½" x 8½". Repeat to make a total of 9 block C.

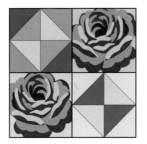

Block C
Make 9.

Assembling the Quilt Top

1. Refer to the quilt assembly diagram to arrange the blocks into eight horizontal rows of six blocks each as shown, placing the lighter blocks toward the center of the quilt and rotating some of the B blocks so the rose square is in the opposite corner. Press the seams in alternate directions from row to row. Sew the rows together. Press the seams in one direction.

2. Refer to "Adding Borders" on page 106 to stitch the rose-print 6½"-wide strips to the quilt top.

Finishing Your Quilt

Refer to "General Instructions," beginning on page 105, for specific instructions for each of the following finishing steps.

1. Layer the quilt top with batting and backing; baste.

2. Quilt in an overall design, using variegated quilting thread to coordinate with your fabrics.

3. Use the 2¾"-wide rose-print strips to bind the quilt edges.

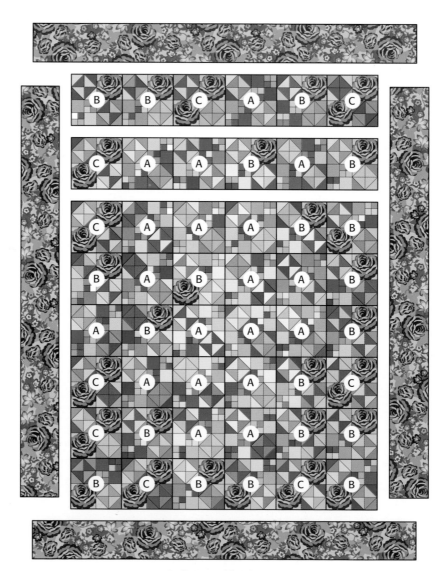

Quilt Assembly Diagram

A Village Tradition: Open Gardens

DURING ONE—HOPEFULLY SUNNY—weekend in June, a number of the local residents host a kind of garden open house called Open Gardens, which benefits the local parish church. The gardens, which are always abundant, are given an early summer trimming and tidying by their owners to prepare them for the many visitors who stroll from garden to garden in the village. Visitors make donations to charities, enjoy tea in the village hall, and take the opportunity to tour the unique garden spots the village has to offer.

Villagers look forward each year to the event, not only to raise money for a worthy cause, but to view each other's beautiful gardens and share a lovely day with friends throughout the village. Definitely a delightful tradition! How about trying this in your own community? Perhaps your quilt guild could use it as a fund-raising event by putting their own twist on it and showcasing colorful quilts in the garden setting. Display quilts on a table with cool lemonade, hang them on the fence for a spot of unexpected color, or spread a few on the grass for visitors to sit on and rest before they visit the next garden. Make it the start of a new quilting tradition!

It's definitely a festive affair—the charming village gardens are open for visitors!

Chain of Ivy

*L*uscious, trailing ivy and other vines are everywhere:

on the garden walls, around the doorways, and climbing on the cottages—

sometimes covering the walls and creeping onto the roofs. They add

an enchanting look to whatever they adorn. Appliquéd trailing ivy

adds the same enchantment to this dramatic Irish Chain quilt.

Multiple shades of rose and blue intertwine to create a

unique twist to a classic favorite.

Materials

Yardage is based on 42"-wide fabric.

- 8½ yards of yellow fabric for blocks and borders
- 3 yards of green fabric for leaf and vine appliqués
- 1⅞ yards total of assorted blue fabrics for blocks
- 1⅝ yards total of assorted rose fabrics for blocks
- 7½ yards of fabric for backing
- ⅞ yard of fabric for binding
- 88" x 118" piece of batting
- ½" bias bar
- Fabric glue stick (optional)
- Freezer paper

Cutting

All measurements include ¼"-wide seam allowances.

From the yellow fabric, cut:

70 strips, 2" x 42"; from 10 of the strips, cut:
    20 strips, 2" x 14"
    4 squares, 2" x 2"

12 strips, 5" x 42"

9 strips, 8½" x 42"

From the assorted blue fabrics, cut a *total* of:

30 strips, 2" x 42"; cut 1 strip into 14 squares, 2" x 2"

From the assorted rose fabrics, cut a *total* of:

27 strips, 2" x 42"; cut 1 strip into 10 squares, 2" x 2"

From the binding fabric, cut:

10 strips, 2¾" x 42"

Chain of Ivy

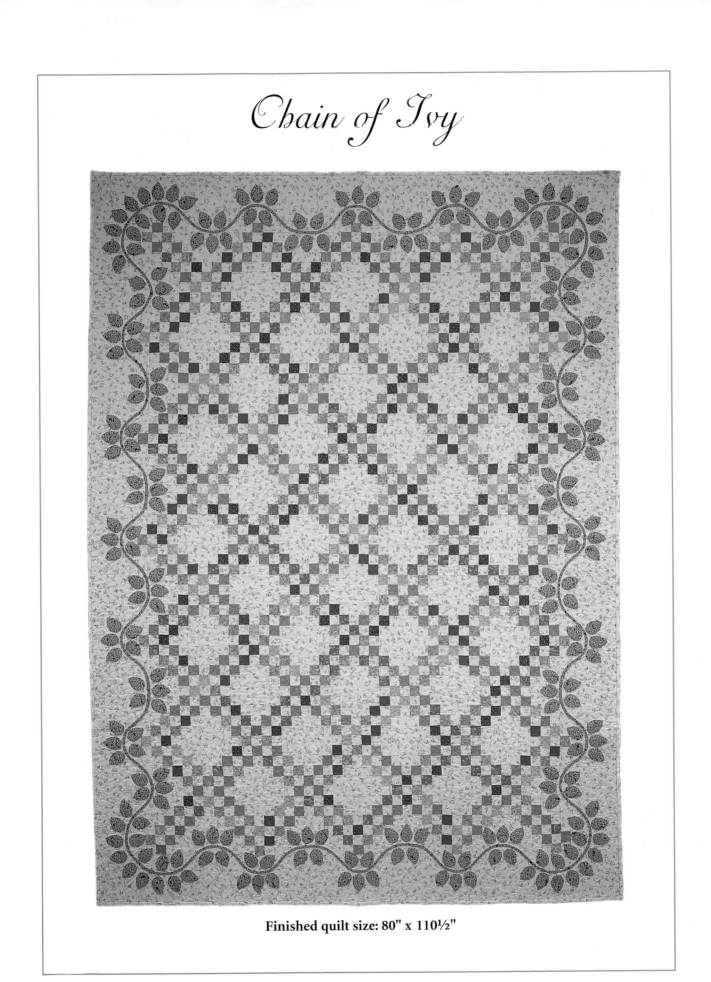

Finished quilt size: 80" x 110½"

Making the Blocks

1. Using yellow, assorted rose, and assorted blue 2" x 42" strips, make strip sets A–G as shown. Make the number indicated for each strip set. Press the seams toward the rose and blue strips. From the strip sets, crosscut the number of 2"-wide segments indicated.

2. Using yellow 5" x 42" strips and yellow, assorted rose, and assorted blue 2" x 42" strips, make strip sets H and I. Make the number indicated for each strip set. Press the seams in the directions indicated. Cut strip set H into 96 segments, 2" wide. Cut strip set I into 38 segments, 5" wide, and 20 segments, 3½" wide.

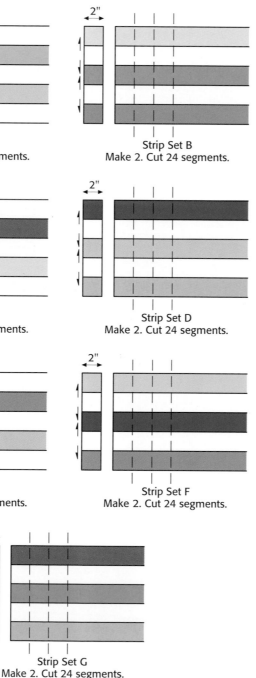

Strip Set A
Make 3. Cut 48 segments.

Strip Set B
Make 2. Cut 24 segments.

Strip Set C
Make 3. Cut 53 segments.

Strip Set D
Make 2. Cut 24 segments.

Strip Set E
Make 3. Cut 48 segments.

Strip Set F
Make 2. Cut 24 segments.

Strip Set G
Make 2. Cut 24 segments.

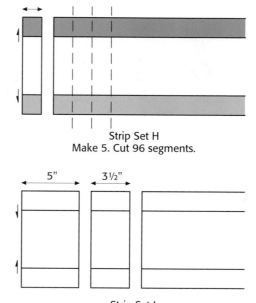

Strip Set H
Make 5. Cut 96 segments.

Strip Set I
Make 7. Cut 38 segments 5" wide.
Cut 20 segments 3½" wide.

3. Using yellow and assorted blue 2" x 42" strips, make one strip set each of J and K. Press the seams toward the blue strips. From the strip sets, crosscut the number of 2"-wide segments indicated.

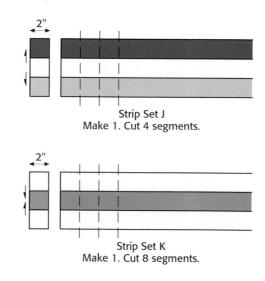

Strip Set J
Make 1. Cut 4 segments.

Strip Set K
Make 1. Cut 8 segments.

4. Stitch the segments from strip sets A–H and the 5"-wide segments from strip set I together as shown to make blocks 1–5 for the quilt top. Make the number indicated for each block. Press the seams in alternate directions from row to row. The blocks should measure 8" x 8".

5. Using the 2"-wide segments from strip sets C, E, F, G, H, J, and K and the 3½"-wide segments from strip set I, make blocks 6–10 for the inner border. Make the number indicated for each block. Press the seams in alternate directions from row to row. Blocks 6–9 should measure 5" x 8" and block 10 should measure 5" x 5".

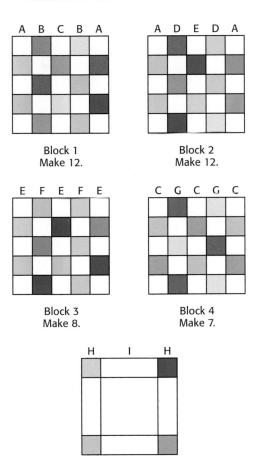

A B C B A

Block 1
Make 12.

A D E D A

Block 2
Make 12.

E F E F E

Block 3
Make 8.

C G C G C

Block 4
Make 7.

H I H

Block 5
Make 38.

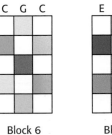

C G C

Block 6
Make 10.

E F E

Block 7
Make 6.

H I

Block 8
Make 10.

H I

Block 9
Make 10.

K J K

Block 10
Make 4.

Assembling the Quilt Top

Refer to the quilt assembly diagram for the following steps.

1. Arrange blocks 1–5 into 11 rows of seven blocks each. Sew the blocks in each row together. Press the seams in alternate directions from row to row. Sew the rows together. Press the seams toward the rows that begin with block 5.

2. Stitch the border blocks together as shown to make the inner border strips. Press the seams toward blocks 8 and 9. Stitch the top and bottom border strips to the top and bottom edges of the quilt top. Stitch the side border strips to the quilt sides.

3. Sew the assorted blue 2" squares, assorted rose 2" squares, yellow 2" squares, and yellow 2" x 14" strips together as shown to make the middle border strips. Press the seams toward the yellow strips. Stitch the top and bottom border strips to the top and bottom edges of the quilt top. Stitch the side border strips to the quilt sides.

4. Refer to "Adding Borders" on page 106 to stitch the yellow 8½" x 42" outer border strips to the quilt top.

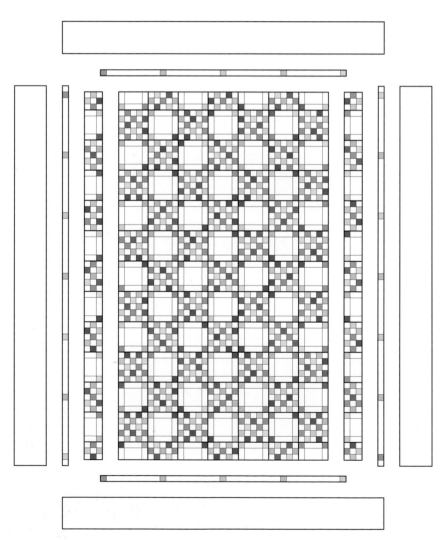

Quilt Assembly Diagram

Adding the Appliqués

1. To make the vine, refer to "Cutting Bias Strips" on page 106 and cut approximately 475" of 1½"-wide bias strips from the green fabric. Sew the strips together end to end to make one long strip. Refer to the manufacturer's instructions to stitch the bias strip into a tube, using the bias bar.

2. Refer to the photograph on page 45 to position the vine, pinning it in place or using the fabric glue stick. Stitch along both edges of the vine using a hand- or invisible machine-appliqué stitch.

3. Refer to "Freezer-Paper Appliqué" on page 105 to prepare 236 leaves for appliqué from the remaining green fabric.

4. Pin or glue the leaves in position along the appliquéd vine, referring to the photo for placement. Stitch along the edges of the leaves, using a hand- or invisible machine-appliqué stitch.

Finishing Your Quilt

Refer to "General Instructions," beginning on page 105, for specific instructions for each of the following finishing steps.

1. Layer the quilt top with batting and backing; baste.

2. Quilt approximately ¹⁄₁₆" to ⅛" from the edges of the appliquéd vine and leaves. Stipple quilt in a tight pattern in the yellow areas of the quilt, leaving the blue and rose chain unquilted.

3. Use the 2¾"-wide binding strips to bind the quilt edges.

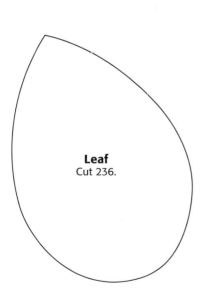

Leaf
Cut 236.

A Proper Garden

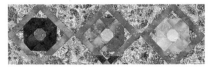

When my family from England visited me in the United States, they were
very pleased to see that I had a "proper English garden." Certainly no street in Nayland
captures the charm of a "proper garden" more than Fenn Street, where not only
does each cottage have a lovely garden but also an enchanting footbridge crossing
the small stream that winds down the street—a perfect place
for this quilt of colorful pieced flowers.

Materials

Yardage is based on 42"-wide fabric.

- 3⅛ yards of floral print for blocks, setting triangles, and second and fourth borders
- ⅝ yard of light purple mottled solid for block borders
- ⅜ yard of yellow mottled solid for first border
- ⅜ yard of dark purple mottled solid for third border
- ⅛ yard each of 12 assorted mottled solids for flower petals and centers
- Scraps of assorted green fabrics for leaves
- 3¾ yards of fabric for backing
- 1 yard of fabric for bias binding
- 65" x 72" piece of batting
- Freezer paper
- Dinner plate for border template

Cutting

All measurements include ¼"-wide seam allowances.

From *each* of the assorted mottled solids for the petals and centers, cut:

5 squares, 2½" x 2½"

2 squares, 2⅞" x 2⅞"

4 squares, 1" x 1"

From the light purple mottled solid, cut:

10 strips, 1½" x 42"; crosscut into:
    36 strips, 1½" x 6½"
    12 strips, 1½" x 7½"
    12 squares, 1½" x 1½"

From the assorted green scraps, cut:

24 rectangles, 1½" x 2½"

From the floral print, cut:

2 strips, 2⅞" x 42"; crosscut into 24 squares, 2⅞" x 2⅞"

2 strips, 8½" x 42"; crosscut into 6 squares, 8½" x 8½"

1 strip, 12¾" x 42"; crosscut into 3 squares, 12¾" x 12¾". Cut each square in half twice diagonally to yield 12 quarter-square triangles. You will use 10 and have 2 left over.

1 strip, 6⅝" x 42"; crosscut into 2 squares, 6⅝" x 6⅝". Cut each square in half once diagonally to yield 4 half-square triangles.

5 strips, 2½" x 42"

7 strips, 6½" x 42"

From the yellow mottled solid, cut:

5 strips, 1½" x 42"

From the dark purple mottled solid, cut:

6 strips, 1½" x 42"

A Proper Garden

Finished quilt size: 54" x 66"

Making the Blocks

1. With a soft-lead pencil, draw a diagonal line from corner to corner on the wrong side of two assorted mottled 2⅞" squares of the same color. Place each of the marked squares right sides together with a floral-print 2⅞" square. Using your presser foot as a guide, stitch ¼" from both sides of the drawn line on each square. Cut along the drawn lines with a scissors to make a total of 4 half-square-triangle units. Press the seams toward the floral-print triangles.

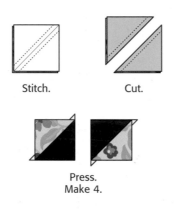

Stitch. Cut.

Press.
Make 4.

2. Draw a diagonal line from corner to corner on the wrong side of four assorted mottled 1" squares of the same color used in step 1. Select a mottled 2½" square in a contrasting color for the flower center. Position the marked squares on each corner of the 2½" square as shown. Stitch on the marked lines. Press the triangles toward the corners.

3. Using the units from steps 1 and 2 and four matching assorted mottled 2½" squares, assemble the block as shown.

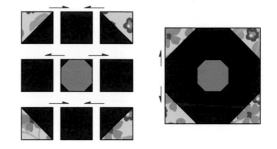

4. Repeat steps 1–3 to make a total of 12 Flower blocks.

5. Sew a light purple 1½" x 6½" strip to the left side of each block and a light purple 1½" x 7½" strip to the top of each block as shown. Press the seams toward the strips.

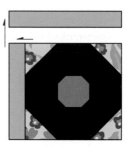

6. Position a green 1½" x 2½" rectangle at the end of a light purple 1½" x 6½" strip, right sides together, as shown. Stitch diagonally from the upper left corner of the green strip to the lower right corner of the purple strip as shown. Trim the seam to ¼". Press the seam toward the purple strips. Make 12.

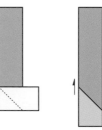

Make 12.

7. Repeat step 6 with the remaining green 1½" x 2½" rectangles and light purple 1½" x 6½" strips, extending the green strip to the left as shown. Stitch diagonally from the upper right corner of the green strip to the lower left corner of the purple strip. Press the seam toward the purple strip. Make 12.

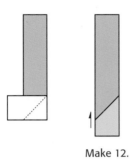

Make 12.

8. Stitch a strip from step 7 to the right-hand side of each block as shown. Press the seams toward the strips. Sew a light purple 1½" square to the end of each strip from step 6. Press the seams toward the strips. Stitch a pieced strip to the bottom of each block. Press the seams toward the strips. The block should measure 8½" x 8½". Make 12 blocks.

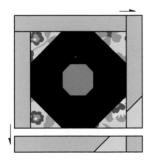

Assembling the Quilt Top

1. Arrange the blocks, the floral 8½" squares, and the floral quarter-square triangles into six diagonal rows as shown. Sew the pieces in each row together. Press the seams toward the floral squares and triangles. Sew the rows together. Press the seams in alternate directions. Stitch the floral half-square triangles to each corner of the quilt top. Press the seams toward the triangles.

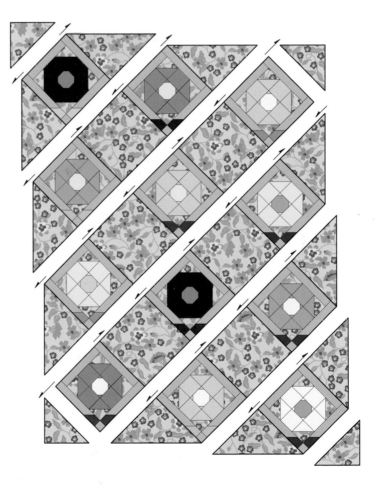

2. Refer to "Adding Borders" on page 106 and the quilt assembly diagram to stitch the yellow 1½" x 42" strips to the quilt top. Repeat with the floral 2½" x 42" strips, followed by the dark purple 1½" x 42" strips, and then the floral 6½" x 42" strips. Press the seams toward the borders after each addition.

3. To scallop the floral outer border, begin by cutting a piece of freezer paper that is the same length and width as the top border and one piece that is the same length and width as a side border.

4. With the dull side of the freezer paper facing up and using a dinner plate as a guide, position the plate in the corner of the top border freezer-paper piece. Trace around the top portion of the plate to make the first corner. For the next scallop, overlap the first scallop as much as you wish and trace around the top portion of the plate. If you want only a slight scallop, overlap a great deal. If you prefer a deeper scalloped edge, position and trace the plate farther from the preceding scallop. Continue along the top until you reach the opposite corner. If the scallops don't come out just as you like, simply redraw them, overlapping more or less until you have just the look you want.

5. With the dull side still facing up, press the freezer paper to the top border. Cut around the scallops through the paper and fabric. Remove the freezer paper.

6. Position the side border freezer-paper strip, dull side up, on the side border. Repeat steps 4 and 5, using the corner scallop from the top as the starting point.

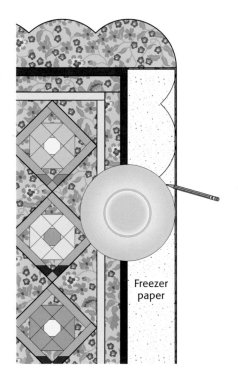

Freezer paper

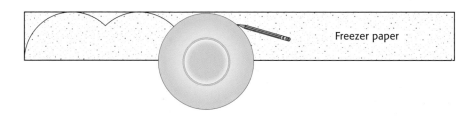

Freezer paper

7. To add scallops to the remaining sides, iron the freezer paper with the drawn scallops that you removed from the top and side to the bottom and remaining side, and cut around the scallops.

Finishing Your Quilt

Refer to "General Instructions," beginning on page 105, for specific instructions for each of the following finishing steps.

1. Layer the quilt top with batting and backing; baste.
2. Quilt the floral blocks and borders in an overall pattern, adding detail to the flowers as desired.
3. Refer to "Cutting Bias Strips" on page 106 to cut approximately 350" of 2½"-wide bias strips. Refer to "Bias Binding" on page 109 to bind the quilt edges.

Quilt Assembly Diagram

Cottage Welcome

I love the cottage doorways in the village. Each one has its own special charm and personality. The colorfully painted doors, surrounded by blooming roses and other vines, entice approaching visitors. They were the inspiration for this welcome banner you can add to your own front doorway.

Materials

Yardage is based on 42"-wide fabric.

- ⅝ yard *total* of assorted peach hand-dyed fabrics for blocks, center square, pieced third border, and berries
- ½ yard *total* of assorted light yellow hand-dyed fabrics for blocks and second and fourth borders
- ½ yard *total* of assorted dark yellow hand-dyed fabrics for blocks and pieced third border
- ½ yard of medium green fabric for fifth border and center circle vine
- ⅛ yard of medium green print for first border
- ⅛ yard of light green fabric for pieced third border
- Assorted green scraps for leaf appliqués
- ¾ yard of fabric for backing
- ½ yard of fabric for facings
- 22" x 33" piece of batting
- ⅜" bias bar
- Fabric glue stick (optional)

Cutting

All measurements include ¼"-wide seam allowances.

From the assorted peach hand-dyed fabrics, cut a *total* of:

8 squares, 1½" x 1½"

4 strips, 1" x 42"; crosscut into:
    8 rectangles, 1" x 1½"
    8 rectangles, 1" x 2"
    8 rectangles, 1" x 2½"
    8 rectangles, 1" x 3"
    8 rectangles, 1" x 3½"
    8 rectangles, 1" x 4"

1 strip, 2⅞" x 42"; crosscut into:
    8 squares, 2⅞" x 2⅞"
    1 square, 8½" x 8½"

From the assorted light yellow hand-dyed fabrics, cut a *total* of:

5 strips, 1" x 42"; crosscut into:
    4 rectangles, 1" x 1½"
    12 rectangles, 1" x 2"
    12 rectangles, 1" x 2½"
    12 rectangles, 1" x 3"
    12 rectangles, 1" x 3½"
    4 rectangles, 1" x 4"

From one of the assorted light yellow hand-dyed fabrics, cut:

2 strips, 1½" x 42"; crosscut into 4 strips, 1½" x 16½"

From the assorted dark yellow hand-dyed fabrics, cut a *total* of:

4 squares, 1½" x 1½"

5 strips, 1" x 42"; crosscut into:
    4 rectangles, 1" x 2"
    4 rectangles, 1" x 2½"
    4 rectangles, 1" x 3"
    4 rectangles, 1" x 3½"
    12 rectangles, 1" x 4"
    12 rectangles, 1" x 4½"

1 strip, 2⅞" x 42"; crosscut into 8 squares, 2⅞" x 2⅞"

From the medium green print for first border, cut:

1 strip, 1½" x 42"; crosscut into 2 strips, 1½" x 16½"

From the light green fabric, cut:

1 strip, 2⅞" x 42"; crosscut into 16 squares, 2⅞" x 2⅞"

From the medium green fabric for fifth border and center circle vine, cut:

1 strip, 2" x 42"; crosscut into 2 strips, 2" x 16½"

From the facing fabric, cut:

3 strips, 2½" x 42"; crosscut into:
    2 strips, 2½" x 27½"
    1 strip, 2½" x 18½"

1 strip, 4½" x 18½"

Cottage Welcome

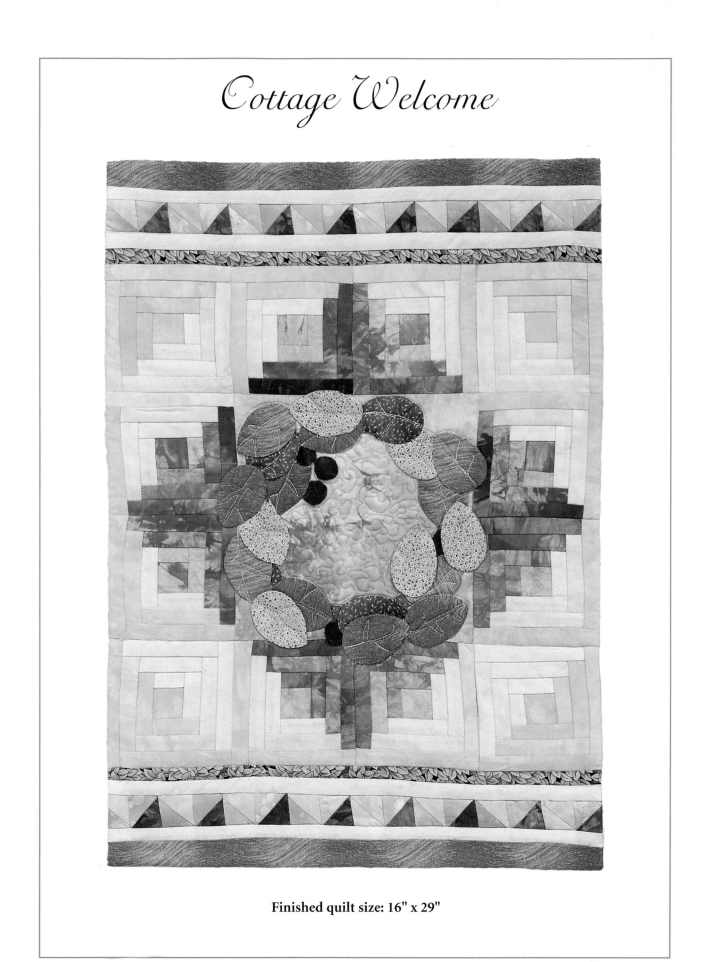

Finished quilt size: 16" x 29"

Making the Blocks

Press the seam allowances toward the newly added strip after each addition.

1. To make the peach-and-yellow Log Cabin blocks, stitch a peach 1" x 1½" rectangle to the left side of each peach 1½" square.

1" x 1½" ⟶ ◀ 1½" x 1½"

2. Sew a peach 1" x 2" rectangle to the top of each unit as shown.

1" x 2"

3. Sew a light yellow 1" x 2" rectangle to the right side of each unit, followed by a light yellow 1" x 2½" rectangle to the bottom of each unit as shown.

1" x 2"

1" x 2½"

4. Stitch a peach 1" x 2½" rectangle to the left side of each unit, followed by a peach 1" x 3" rectangle to the top of each unit as shown.

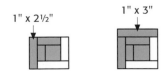

1" x 2½"   1" x 3"

5. Sew a light yellow 1" x 3" rectangle to the right side of each unit, followed by a light yellow 1" x 3½" rectangle to the bottom of each unit as shown.

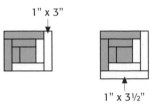

1" x 3"

1" x 3½"

6. Sew a peach 1" x 3½" rectangle to the left side of each unit, followed by a peach 1" x 4" rectangle to the top of each unit as shown.

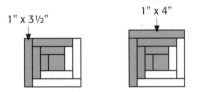

1" x 3½"   1" x 4"

7. Sew a dark yellow 1" x 4" rectangle to the right side of each unit, followed by a dark yellow 1" x 4½" rectangle to the bottom of each unit as shown to complete the blocks. Make 8.

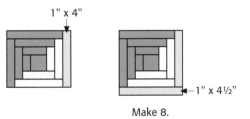

1" x 4"

1" x 4½"

Make 8.

8. Repeat steps 1–7 with the light yellow and dark yellow strips and the dark yellow squares to make four of the blocks shown.

Make 4.

Assembling the Quilt Top

1. Position the Log Cabin blocks and the peach 8½" square into 3 horizontal rows as shown. Sew the blocks in each row together, alternating the pressing direction from row to row. Sew the rows together.

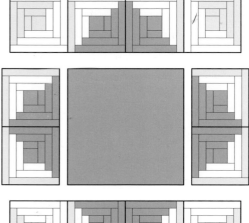

2. Sew a medium green print 1½" x 16½" strip and a light yellow 1½" x 16½" strip to the top and bottom of the quilt top as shown.

3. To make the pieced border, with a soft-lead pencil draw a diagonal line from corner to corner on the wrong side of each light green 2⅞" square. Place a marked square right sides together with each dark yellow 2⅞" square and each peach 2⅞" square. Using your presser foot as a guide, stitch ¼" from both sides of the drawn line on each square. Cut along the drawn lines with a scissors to make a total of 16 green-and-peach half-square-triangle units and 16 green-and-yellow half-square-triangle units. Press the seams toward the peach and yellow triangles.

Make 16.   Make 16.

4. Sew eight green-and-peach units and eight green-and-yellow units together as shown. Make 2. Refer to the quilt assembly diagram on page 64 to stitch the strips to the top and bottom edges of the quilt top.

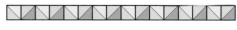

Make 2.

5. Sew the remaining light yellow 1½" x 16½" strips and then the medium green 2" x 16½" strips to the top and bottom edges of the quilt top.

Quilt Assembly Diagram

Adding the Appliqués

1. To make the vine, refer to "Cutting Bias Strips" on page 106 to cut approximately 30" of 1¼"-wide bias strips from the remaining medium green fabric. Sew the strips together end to end to make one long strip. Refer to the manufacturer's instructions to stitch the bias strip into a tube, using the bias bar.

2. Arrange the tube in a circle, approximately 7" in diameter, on the center peach square. Pin or use the glue stick to secure the vine in place. Stitch along both long edges of the vine, using a hand- or invisible machine-appliqué stitch.

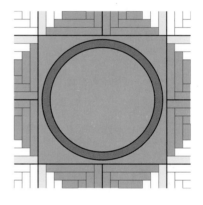

3. Referring to "Freezer-Paper Appliqué" on page 105 and using the patterns on page 66, prepare 20 leaves from the assorted green scraps and five berries from the darkest peach fabric. Referring to the appliqué placement guide, position the leaves and berries around the vine circle,

pinning or gluing them in place as you go. Machine or hand appliqué each leaf and berry in place.

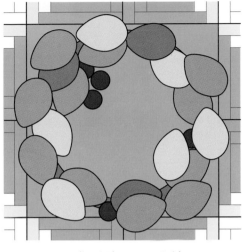

Appliqué Placement Guide

Finishing Your Quilt

Refer to "General Instructions," beginning on page 105, for specific instructions for each of the following finishing steps.

1. Layer the quilt top with batting and backing; baste.
2. Quilt through the center of the appliquéd leaves, making center and side vein lines as shown. Quilt $\frac{1}{16}$" to $\frac{1}{8}$" from the edges of the leaves. Quilt in the wreath center with a small stippling stitch. Stitch in the ditch between the Log Cabin blocks and in the border seams.

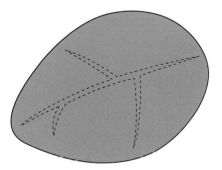

3. Trim the backing and batting even with the quilt top.

4. To add facings to the quilt, with right sides together and raw edges even, pin the 2½" x 27½" facing strips to the sides of the quilt top and sew with a ¼" seam.

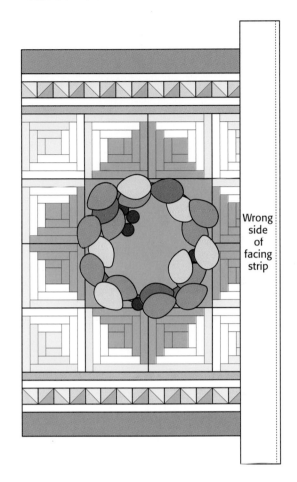

Wrong side of facing strip

5. From the front of the quilt, press the strips outward. Topstitch the facing strips ⅛" from the seam through all layers.

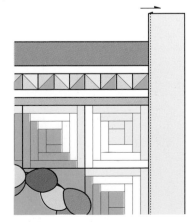

Topstitch ⅛" from seam through all layers.

6. Fold the facings to the back of the quilt so that a slight edge of the quilt top rolls to the back. Press, using steam. Turn the facing raw edges under ¼" and hand stitch to the backing.

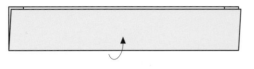

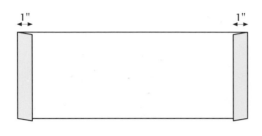

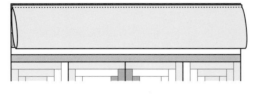

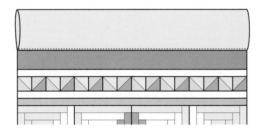

4–6 to stitch the rod pocket to the top edge of the quilt top. Hand stitch the bottom edge of the rod pocket to the quilt back.

7. Repeat steps 4–6 to add the 2½" x 18½" facing strips to the bottom edge of the quilt top, extending the strips 1" beyond the sides. Fold the extensions to the back of the facing strips before stitching down the facings.

8. To add the rod pocket, press the ends of the 4½" x 18½" facing strip under 1". Press the strip in half lengthwise, wrong sides together. Repeat steps

Leaf
Cut 20.

Berry
Cut 5.

Each doorway in the village seems to have its own charm and personality—whether it's surrounded by lush vines or graced with a handful of blossoms at one side. Even the familiar British phone booth has its own welcoming "doorway"!

Lavender Tea

There is something elegant and relaxing about the whole event of afternoon tea.

I find myself being swept away to a fantasy time of less hustle and hurry

and more time to enjoy. It's a ritual I try to squeeze back into my own world, too.

Grace your own tea table with this eye-catching table quilt

that is the perfect backdrop for your favorite teapot and china teacups.

Materials

Yardage is based on 42"-wide fabric.

- 1⅛ yards total of assorted medium and dark purple fabrics
- 2⅜ yards total of assorted light and medium green fabrics
- ⅝ yard of medium green #2 for outer border
- ⅜ yard of light green for inner border
- ⅜ yard of medium green #1 for middle border
- ¼ yard of dark purple for center squares
- 3⅝ yards of fabric for backing
- ¾ yard of fabric for binding
- 64" x 64" square of batting

Choosing Your Fabrics

For this lively quilt, the more fabrics you use, the better. Cut each strip from a different fabric or cut the strips in half to make them about 21" and double the number of half strips. Add a wide range of shades of each color. Don't be afraid to add light and bright fabrics or dark and soft ones. A colorful mix will give your quilt that added pizzazz!

Cutting

All measurements include ¼"-wide seam allowances.

From the assorted purple fabrics, cut a *total* of:

28 strips, 1¼" x 42"; crosscut into:
    48 rectangles, 1¼" x 2"
    48 rectangles, 1¼" x 2¾"
    48 rectangles, 1¼" x 3½"
    48 rectangles, 1¼" x 4¼"
    48 rectangles, 1¼" x 5"
    48 rectangles, 1¼" x 5¾"

From the assorted green fabrics, cut a *total* of:

57 strips, 1¼" x 42"; crosscut into:
    16 rectangles, 1¼" x 2"
    80 rectangles, 1¼" x 2¾"
    80 rectangles, 1¼" x 3½"
    80 rectangles, 1¼" x 4¼"
    80 rectangles, 1¼" x 5"
    80 rectangles, 1¼" x 5¾"
    64 rectangles, 1¼" x 6½"

16 squares, 2" x 2"

From the dark purple for center squares, cut:

3 strips, 2" x 42"; crosscut into 48 squares, 2" x 2"

From the light green for inner border, cut:

5 strips, 1½" x 42"

From the medium green #1 fabric, cut:

6 strips, 1½" x 42"

From the medium green #2 fabric, cut:

6 strips, 2½" x 42"

From the binding fabric, cut:

7 strips, 2¾" x 42"

Lavender Tea

Finished quilt size: 56" x 56"

Making the Blocks

Vary the fabric shades within the blocks for a variegated look. To make some blocks light or dark, use all light or dark shades of green or purple within a block. Press the seam allowances toward the newly added strip after each addition.

1. Set aside four light green 2" squares and four light green rectangles of each length to use for the center blocks.
2. To make the green-and-purple Log Cabin blocks, stitch a purple 1¼" x 2" rectangle to the right side of each dark purple 2" square.

2" x 2" → ← 1¼" x 2"

3. Sew a purple 1¼" x 2¾" rectangle to the bottom of each unit as shown.

1¼" x 2¾"

4. Sew a green 1¼" x 2¾" rectangle to the left side of each unit, followed by a green 1¼" x 3½" rectangle to the top of each unit as shown.

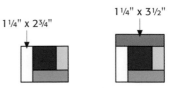

1¼" x 2¾"   1¼" x 3½"

5. Stitch a purple 1¼" x 3½" rectangle to the right side of each unit, followed by a purple 1¼" x 4¼" rectangle to the bottom of each unit as shown.

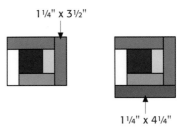

1¼" x 3½"

1¼" x 4¼"

6. Sew a green 1¼" x 4¼" rectangle to the left side of each unit, followed by a green 1¼" x 5" rectangle to the top of each unit as shown.

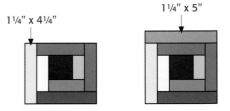

1¼" x 4¼"   1¼" x 5"

7. Stitch a purple 1¼" x 5" rectangle to the right side of each unit, followed by a purple 1¼" x 5¾" rectangle to the bottom of each unit as shown.

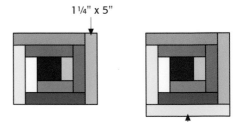

1¼" x 5"

1¼" x 5¾"

8. Sew a green 1¼" x 5¾" rectangle to the left side of each unit, followed by a green 1¼" x 6½" rectangle to the top of each unit as shown to complete the blocks. Make 48.

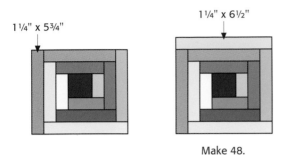

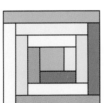

Make 48.

9. Repeat steps 2–8 with the remaining assorted green rectangles, making four of the blocks with the light green squares and rectangles you set aside in step 1. Make 16 total.

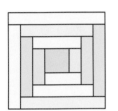

Make 4.   Make 12.

Assembling the Quilt Top

1. To make unit A, arrange four purple-and-green Log Cabin blocks in two rows of two blocks each. Stitch the rows together. Press the seams in alternate directions from row to row. Sew the rows together. Repeat to make 12 of unit A.

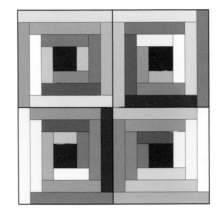

Unit A
Make 12.

2. To make unit B, repeat step 1, using four green Log Cabin blocks, one of which should be a block that was made from all light green strips. Make 4 of unit B.

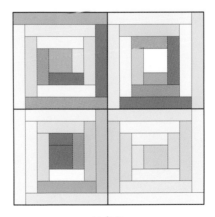

Unit B
Make 4.

3. Refer to the quilt assembly diagram to arrange the A and B units into four horizontal rows of four units each as shown. Be sure to place the B units so the light green squares are in the center of the quilt top. Stitch the units in each row together. Press the seams in alternate directions from row to row. Sew the rows together. Press the seams in one direction.

4. Refer to "Adding Borders" on page 106 and the quilt assembly diagram to stitch the light green inner border strips to the quilt top. Repeat with the medium green #1 middle border strips and then the medium green #2 outer border strips.

Finishing Your Quilt

Refer to "General Instructions," beginning on page 105 for specific instructions for each of the following finishing steps.

1. Layer the quilt top with batting and backing; baste.
2. Quilt an allover pattern using a variegated purple-and-green thread.
3. Use the 2¾"-wide binding strips to bind the quilt edges.

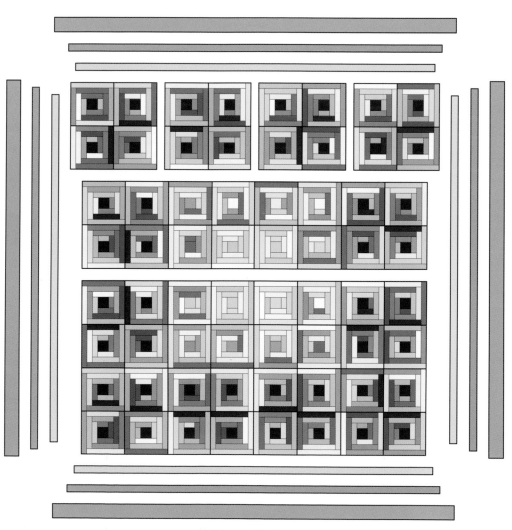

Quilt Assembly Diagram

Afternoon Tea

IT'S A LOVELY ENGLISH TRADITION. Whenever there is something to share or celebrate, out comes a pot of tea. It might be wonderful family news, a meeting of old friends, or even less-than-happy times. Whatever the occasion, you'll find people enjoying the ritual of tea. Afternoon tea is served late in the day, perhaps at four or five o'clock. It has been a revered English custom for centuries, both at home and in tea shops that can be found everywhere from country villages to elegant city surroundings. With today's ever-faster pace of life, the daily routine of afternoon tea may have fallen off slightly, but it still plays an important role.

Tea isn't the only essential item served at this customary gathering. Tasty treats also are part of the tradition. Afternoon tea should begin with delicate sandwiches, such as cucumber or egg, served without the crusts, of course. Then come the delicious cakes—sweet, but not too sweet. All enjoyed with tea, often taken with a little milk.

Try this delightful English tradition yourself and capture a few moments of sharing and conversation with friends or family at the end of a busy day. Choose your favorite tea, bring out your most elegant china teacups and vintage napkins, and set your table. For afternoon tea, start with small cucumber sandwiches. Then serve this delicious Lavender Tea Cake among your own favorite sweets.

Lavender Tea Cake

- 1 cup butter
- 1 cup sugar
- 3 eggs
- 1½ cups flour
- 1 teaspoon baking powder
- 1½ teaspoons dried, minced lavender blossoms
- ½ teaspoon vanilla
- 2 tablespoons milk
- ½ cup confectioner's sugar
- ½ tablespoon water
- Fresh lavender (for garnish)

Preheat oven to 350°. Grease and flour a 9"-round or 9"-square pan. Cream the butter and sugar until fluffy. Add the eggs and beat until the mixture is smooth and glossy. Fold in flour, baking powder, lavender blossoms, vanilla, and milk. Pour the mixture into the prepared pan and bake for 35 minutes. Let cool. Remove from pan and place on serving platter.

Mix the confectioner's sugar and water together. Drizzle over the cake and garnish with fresh lavender.

*J*ust like traditional blue-and-white English china, this blue-and-white quilt

has a sense of classic elegance. Covering the table in front of this amazing

14th-century fireplace, it adds a sense of warmth and a touch of color

to the cozy meal that will be enjoyed in this inviting setting.

Materials

Yardage is based on 42"-wide fabric.

- **Fabric 1:** 1¾ yards of light blue print for blocks A and B
- **Fabric 2:** ¾ yard of dark blue for block A
- **Fabric 3:** 1¼ yards of medium blue print for block A, block B, and first border
- **Fabric 4:** ¼ yard of light blue for block A
- **Fabric 5:** ⅞ yard of dark blue print for block A
- **Fabric 6:** ⅝ yard of blue check for block B
- **Fabric 7:** 2 yards of blue large floral print for block B and second and third borders
- **Fabric 8:** 1½ yards of blue small floral print for third and fourth borders
- 1¾ yards of white print for block A, block B, and first border
- ⅝ yard of yellow print for block B
- 7⅜ yards of fabric for backing
- ⅞ yard of fabric for binding
- 88" x 88" square of batting

Cutting

All measurements include ¼"-wide seam allowances.

From fabric 1, cut:

3 strips, 4½" x 42"; crosscut into 48 rectangles, 2½" x 4½"

5 strips, 3⅜" x 42"; crosscut into 52 squares, 3⅜" x 3⅜"

2 strips, 2⅞" x 42"; crosscut into 26 squares, 2⅞" x 2⅞". Cut each square in half once diagonally to yield 52 half-square triangles.

6 strips, 2½" x 42"; crosscut into 96 squares, 2½" x 2½"

From fabric 2, cut:

6 strips, 2⅞" x 42"; crosscut into 78 squares, 2⅞" x 2⅞". Cut each square in half once diagonally to yield 156 half-square triangles.

From fabric 3, cut:

4 strips, 4½" x 42"; crosscut into 60 rectangles, 2½" x 4½"

4 strips, 2⅞" x 42"; crosscut into 52 squares, 2⅞" x 2⅞". Cut each square in half once diagonally to yield 104 half-square triangles.

1 strip, 2½" x 42"; crosscut into 16 squares, 2½" x 2½"

From fabric 4, cut:

2 strips, 3⅜" x 42"; crosscut into 13 squares, 3⅜" x 3⅜"

From fabric 5, cut:

5 strips, 3⅜" x 42"; crosscut into 52 squares, 3⅜" x 3⅜"

3 strips, 2⅞" x 42"; crosscut into 26 squares, 2⅞" x 2⅞". Cut each square in half once diagonally to yield 52 half-square triangles.

From fabric 6, cut:

6 strips, 2½" x 42"; crosscut into 96 squares, 2½" x 2½"

From fabric 7, cut:

14 strips, 4½" x 42"; crosscut 6 strips into:
   72 rectangles, 2½" x 4½"
   12 squares, 4½" x 4½"

From fabric 8, cut:

18 strips, 2½" x 42"; crosscut 10 strips into 148 squares, 2½" x 2½"

From the white print, cut:

4 strips, 2⅞" x 42"; crosscut into 52 squares, 2⅞" x 2⅞". Cut each square in half once diagonally to yield 104 half-square triangles.

15 strips, 2½" x 42"; crosscut into:
   120 squares, 2½" x 2½"
   12 rectangles, 2½" x 4½"
   16 rectangles, 2½" x 8½"
   4 rectangles, 2½" x 6½"

From the yellow print, cut:

6 strips, 2½" x 42"; crosscut into 96 squares, 2½" x 2½"

From the binding fabric, cut:

9 strips, 2¾" x 42"

China Blue

Finished quilt size: 80" x 80"

Making the Blocks

1. **To make block A,** sew one fabric 2 triangle and one fabric 3 triangle to opposite sides of a 3⅜" fabric 1 square as shown. Press the seams toward the triangles. Repeat to sew a fabric 2 and fabric 3 triangle to the remaining two sides of the square. The unit should measure 4½" square. Make 4.

Make 4.

2. Repeat step 1 to sew four fabric 2 triangles to a fabric 4 square. Make 1.

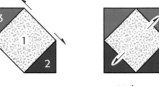

Make 1.

3. Repeat step 1 to sew two white triangles, one fabric 5 triangle, and one fabric 1 triangle to a fabric 5 square. Make 4.

Make 4.

4. Arrange the units from steps 1–3 into 3 horizontal rows as shown. Stitch the units in each row together. Press the seams in alternate directions from row to row. Stitch the rows together. Press the seams in one direction. The block should measure 12½" x 12½".

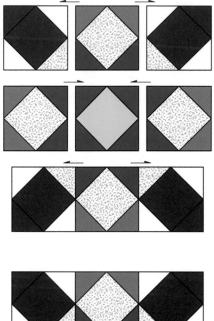

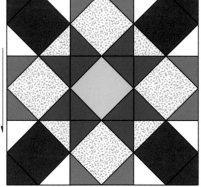

Block A

5. Repeat steps 1–4 to make a total of 13 block A.

6. **To make block B,** stitch eight white and eight yellow squares together in pairs. Sew the pairs together as shown to make four four-patch units.

Make 4.

7. Draw a diagonal line on the wrong side of eight 2½" fabric 1 squares. With right sides together, place a marked square on one end of four fabric 3 rectangles. Stitch on the drawn line. Trim the fabric 1 square ¼" from the stitching line. Press fabric 1 toward the corner. Place the remaining squares on the opposite corner of each rectangle and repeat the stitching and trimming process.

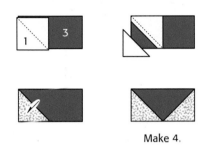

Make 4.

8. Repeat step 7 to make four units with the fabric 1 rectangles and the fabric 6 squares.

Make 4.

9. Sew the units from steps 7 and 8 together in pairs as shown to make four flying-geese units.

Make 4.

10. Arrange the four-patch units from step 6, the flying-geese units from step 9, and a fabric 7 square into three horizontal rows. Stitch the units in each row together. Press the seams in alternate directions from row to row. Sew the rows together. The block should measure 12½" x 12½".

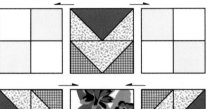

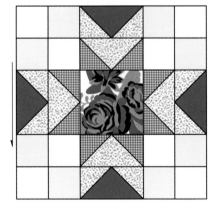

Block B

11. Repeat steps 6–10 to make a total of 12 block B.

Assembling the Quilt Top

1. Alternately arrange blocks A and B into five horizontal rows of five blocks each as shown. Stitch the blocks in each row together. Press the seams in alternate directions from row to row. Stitch the rows together. Press the seams in one direction.

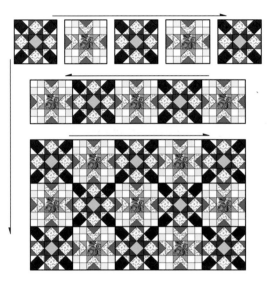

2. Draw a diagonal line on the wrong side of 24 white squares. With right sides together, place a marked square on one end of 12 fabric 3 rectangles. Stitch on the drawn line. Trim the white square ¼" from the stitching line. Press the white triangle toward the corner. Place the remaining squares on the opposite corner of each rectangle and repeat the stitching and trimming process.

Make 12.

3. Repeat step 2 to make eight units with the 2½" x 4½" white rectangles and the fabric 3 squares.

Make 8.

4. To assemble the first border, sew two white 2½" x 4½" rectangles, three units from step 2, two units from step 3, and four white 2½" x 8½" rectangles together as shown. Press the seams toward the rectangles. Make 2. Refer to the quilt assembly diagram to stitch the strips to the sides of the quilt top as shown.

2½" x 8½"

2½" x 4½"

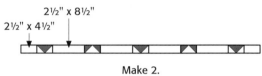

Make 2.

5. Repeat step 4 to make two strips, substituting the white 2½" x 6½" rectangles for the 2½" x 4½" rectangles. Refer to the quilt assembly diagram to stitch the strips to the top and bottom edges of the quilt top.

2½" x 6½"

Make 2.

6. Refer to "Adding Borders" on page 106 to add the 4½" x 42" fabric 7 strips to the quilt.

7. Refer to step 2 to make 72 units with the fabric 7 rectangles and the fabric 8 squares.

Make 72.

8. To assemble the third border, stitch the units from step 7 into four strips with 19 units each. Make sure all of

the points are pointing in the same direction. Refer to the quilt assembly diagram to stitch two strips to the sides of the quilt top. Press the seams toward the second border. Stitch a fabric 8 square to the ends of the two remaining strips. Stitch the strips to the top and bottom edges of the quilt top. Press the seams toward the second border.

9. Refer to "Adding Borders" on page 106 to stitch the 2½"-wide fabric 8 strips to the quilt top.

Finishing Your Quilt

Refer to "General Instructions," beginning on page 105, for specific instructions for each of the following finishing steps.

1. Layer the quilt top with batting and backing; baste.
2. Machine or hand quilt in an allover pattern.
3. Use the 2¾"-wide binding strips to bind the quilt edges.

Quilt Assembly Diagram

Cottage Rose

*T*his area of the English countryside is well known for its beautiful roses.

In early summer when they are in full bloom, their fragrance fills the air

and their gorgeous blooms adorn the doorways and garden walls as we stroll

through the village. To capture the sweet essence of roses, choose a

rose-covered fabric to make this striking lap-size quilt.

Materials

Yardage is based on 42"-wide fabric.

- 2¼ yards of rose print for blocks
- 1¾ yards of peach print for outer border
- 1⅝ yards of dark rose fabric for sashing and binding
- 1⅜ yards of white fabric for blocks and bias strips
- 1 yard of green fabric for blocks and inner border
- ¼ yard of plaid fabric for sashing squares
- 3⅜ yards of fabric for backing
- 60" x 73" piece of batting

Cutting

All measurements include ¼"-wide seam allowances.

From the green fabric, cut:

7 strips, 2⅞" x 42"; crosscut into 80 squares, 2⅞" x 2⅞"

7 strips, 1½" x 42"

From the white fabric, cut:

7 strips, 2⅞" x 42"; crosscut into 80 squares, 2⅞" x 2⅞"

From the rose print, cut:

3 strips, 14⅜" x 42"; crosscut into 5 squares, 14⅜" x 14⅜". Cut each square in half once diagonally to yield 10 half-square triangles.

1 strip, 8¾" x 42"; crosscut into 2 squares, 8¾" x 8¾". Cut each square in half once diagonally to yield 4 half-square triangles.

2 strips, 8½" x 42"; crosscut into 8 squares, 8½" x 8½"

From the dark rose fabric, cut:

12 strips, 2" x 42"; crosscut into 48 rectangles, 2" x 8½"

From the plaid fabric, cut:

2 strips, 2" x 42"; crosscut into 31 squares, 2" x 2"

From the peach fabric, cut:

7 strips, 4½" x 42"

Cottage Rose

Finished quilt size: 52" x 65"

Making the Blocks

1. With a soft-lead pencil, draw a diagonal line from corner to corner on the wrong side of the 80 white squares. Place each of the marked squares right sides together with a green square. Using your presser foot as a guide, stitch ¼" from both sides of the drawn line on each square. Cut along the drawn lines with a scissors to make a total of 160 half-square-triangle units. Press the seams toward the green triangles.

Make 160.

2. Arrange 16 half-square-triangle units from step 1 into 4 horizontal rows of 4 units each as shown. Stitch the units in each row together. Press the seams in alternate directions from row to row. Sew the rows together. Press the seams in one direction. The block should measure 8½" x 8½". Repeat to make a total of 10 blocks.

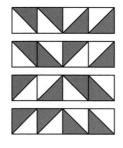 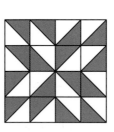

Make 10.

Assembling the Quilt Top

1. Sew the pieced blocks, the rose-print squares, and the dark rose rectangles together to make six block rows as shown. Press the seams in alternate directions from row to row. Stitch the remaining dark rose rectangles and the plaid squares together to make seven sashing rows as shown. Press the seams toward the rectangles. Stitch the sashing rows and the rose-print 14⅜" half-square triangles to the block rows as shown to complete each row. The outer edge of the triangles is cut on the bias, so be sure to handle them carefully so you don't stretch them. Stitch the rows together, and then add the rose-print 8¾" half-square triangles to the corners.

2. Refer to "Adding Borders" on page 106 and the quilt assembly diagram to add the green strips and then the peach strips to the quilt top.

Quilt Assembly Diagram

Finishing Your Quilt

Refer to "General Instructions," beginning on page 105, for specific instructions for each of the following finishing steps.

1. Layer the quilt top with batting and backing; baste.
2. Quilt in the ditch in the pieced blocks and sashing. Quilt an allover floral pattern in the solid blocks and borders.

3. For rounded corners, place a dinner-size plate on each corner and trace around the edge with a pencil. Cut on the pencil lines.

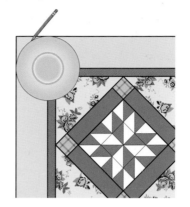

4. Refer to "Cutting Bias Strips" on page 106 to cut approximately 250" of 1"-wide bias strips from the remaining white fabric. Stitch the strips together end to end to make one long strip. Press the strip in half lengthwise, wrong sides together. With raw edges even and using a scant ¼"-wide seam, baste the bias strip to the edge of the quilt, easing it rather than stretching it to fit around the corners. After binding the quilt edge, the folded edge of the white trim will lie against the quilt, just as you have basted it.
5. Refer to "Cutting Bias Strips" on page 106 to cut approximately 250" of 2"-wide bias strips from the remaining dark rose fabric. Stitch the strips together end to end to make one long strip. Refer to "Bias Binding" on page 109 to bind the quilt edges.

Liberty Blossoms

*W*hen I think of classic English style, the first images that come to mind

are the beautiful prints from Liberty of London with their timeless charm.

I purchased the Liberty fabrics for this quilt on one of my first trips to England,

so it has special sentimental appeal for me. This traditional bed-size quilt

will be lovely in any favorite prints of yours as well.

Materials

Yardage is based on 42"-wide fabric.

- 2⅜ yards of green print for blocks, sashing, and first and second borders
- 1¾ yards of yellow floral print for blocks and third border
- ⅜ yard of rose fabric for sashing squares
- 1⅝ yards of yellow fabric for sashing and fourth border
- ¾ yard of white fabric for second border
- 1⅜ yards of paisley print for fifth border
- 5¼ yards of fabric for backing
- ¾ yard of fabric for binding
- 74" x 90" piece of batting

Cutting

All measurements include ¼"-wide seam allowances.

From the yellow floral print, cut:

6 strips, 6½" x 42"; crosscut into 35 squares, 6½" x 6½"

6 strips, 2½" x 42"

Make It to Fit

It's easy to make this quilt larger if you wish. Simply add alternating blocks to the horizontal rows to make it wider, or add another row at the bottom to make it longer. For each vertical or horizontal block you add, increase the triangle border units by two and adjust the other border lengths as needed.

From the green print, cut:

4 strips, 4½" x 42"; crosscut into 52 rectangles, 2½" x 4½"

6 strips, 3½" x 42"; crosscut into 68 squares, 3½" x 3½"

11 strips, 2½" x 42"; crosscut into 164 squares, 2½" x 2½"

6 strips, 1½" x 42"

From the yellow fabric, cut:

6 strips, 6½" x 42"; crosscut into 82 rectangles, 2½" x 6½"

7 strips, 1½" x 42"

From the rose print, cut:

3 strips, 2½" x 42"; crosscut into 48 squares, 2½" x 2½"

From the white fabric, cut:

7 strips, 2½" x 42"; crosscut into 108 squares, 2½" x 2½"

From the paisley print, cut:

7 strips, 6" x 42"

From the binding fabric, cut:

8 strips, 2¾" x 42"

Making the Blocks and Sashing Units

1. To make the blocks, use a soft-lead pencil to draw a diagonal line from corner to corner on the wrong side of each green 3½" square. With right sides together, place a marked square in opposite corners of each of 17 yellow floral squares as shown on page 94. Stitch on the drawn line. Trim the green squares ¼" from the stitching lines. Press the green triangles toward the corners. Place the

Liberty Blossoms

Finished quilt size: 66" x 82"

remaining green squares on the opposite corners of each floral square and repeat the stitching and trimming process.

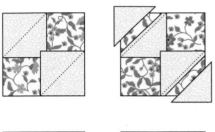
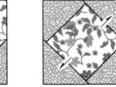

Make 17.

2. To make the sashing units, draw a diagonal line from corner to corner on the wrong side of each green 2½" square. With right sides together, place a marked square on each end of each yellow rectangle. Stitch on the drawn lines. Trim the green squares ¼" from the stitching lines. Press the green triangles toward the corners.

Make 82.

Assembling the Quilt Top

1. To make the sashing rows, sew five sashing units and six rose-print squares together as shown. Press the seams to the left. Make 8.

Make 8.

2. To make block row A, sew two blocks, three yellow floral squares, and six sashing units together as shown. Press the seams to the right. Make 4.

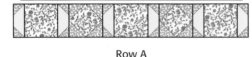

Row A
Make 4.

3. To make block row B, sew three blocks, two yellow floral squares, and six sashing units together as shown. Press the seams to the right. Make 3.

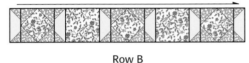

Row B
Make 3.

4. Arrange the sashing rows and A and B block rows as shown.

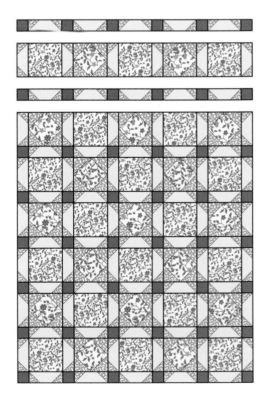

5. Refer to "Adding Borders" on page 106 to stitch the green 1½"-wide strips to the quilt top.

6. To make the pieced border, draw a diagonal line from corner to corner on the wrong side of each white square. With right sides together, place a marked square on one end of each green rectangle. Stitch on the drawn lines. Trim the white squares ¼" from the stitching lines. Press the white triangles toward the corners. Place the remaining squares on the opposite corner of each rectangle and repeat the stitching and trimming process.

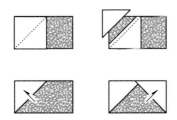

Make 52.

7. Sew 15 units from step 6 together end to end with the points facing in the same direction. Make 2. Refer to the quilt assembly diagram to stitch the strips to the sides of the quilt top. Press the seams toward the first border. Sew 11 units from step 6 together in the same manner. Sew a white square to the ends of the strip. Make 2. Stitch the strips to the top and bottom edges of the quilt top. Press the seams toward the first border.

Side Border
Make 2.

Top/Bottom Border
Make 2.

8. Refer to "Adding Borders" on page 106 and the quilt assembly diagram to stitch the 2½"-wide yellow floral strips to the quilt top, followed by the 1½"-wide yellow strips and then the 6"-wide paisley strips.

Finishing Your Quilt

Refer to "General Instructions," beginning on page 105, for specific instructions for each of the following finishing steps.

1. Layer the quilt top with batting and backing; baste.
2. Quilt as desired.
3. Use the 2¾"-wide binding strips to bind the quilt edges.

Quilt Assembly Diagram

Tradition with a Twist

Durham Quilting

ENGLAND, like the United States, has its own quilting traditions. Perhaps one of the best known, and most admired, of these is Durham quilting, the art of hand quilting allover designs on dramatic whole-cloth quilts and other quilted projects created from elegant fabrics such as sateens, silks, and satins.

The roots of Durham quilting can be found in northern England, where the traditional designs were handed down from mother to daughter for centuries. Industrious women from County Durham were able to find markets for their quilted works in the city of London to help them fight the poverty that afflicted their lives. Their resourcefulness helped to spread the admiration for this unique style of hand quilting.

Although we greatly admire the beauty and tradition of Durham quilting, today few quilters have the time to spend hundreds of hours hand quilting one of these heirloom-style quilts. We can, however, do the next best thing and re-create that same look using our own contemporary tools and timesaving techniques.

Many quilters enjoy machine quilting, and today's sewing machines make it easy to do. Others don't enjoy doing their own machine quilting, so they hire professional machine quilters to do it for them. In either case, you can create lovely whole-cloth designs in the tradition of Durham quilting by using machine quilting—a wonderful combination of yesterday's tradition and today's techniques!

Garden Pillows

BEGIN BY FINDING an eye-catching quilting design. For small- or medium-size pillows, 12" to 16" square, medallions or flower designs work well. For quilting inspiration, try quilting stencils, quilting books, or online sources. Don't worry about the size of the design fitting the pillows. For this project, we will make the pillows fit the quilting design!

Once you've picked the designs, you're ready to select the fabric. Traditional Durham quilting was often done on very elegant fabrics, such as satins and silks, but today's cottons will be just as lovely and will be easy to launder as well. Select several lively shades that will look nice together and buy enough to allow an additional 3" on all sides of your design. For example, if a quilting pattern that you want to use is 12" square, make sure that you cut at least an 18" square of fabric. You can easily trim the square after the quilting is complete if you want a smaller pillow.

Next, trace or stencil the design on your fabric with a water-soluble marker or chalk. Layer the stenciled square with backing and batting, each cut several inches larger than the pillow top on all sides. Machine quilt around the design, using thread that matches the design to create a "traditional" look for your quilted pillows. Trim the batting and backing the same size as the top.

Add matching piping around the edge for a finishing touch. Cut the back the same size as the trimmed pillow top. With right sides together, stitch ½" from the outer edges, leaving about 6" for turning. Turn and press. Stuff lightly and hand stitch the opening closed.

Cobblestones

*J*ust like the stone walkways that wind through the village, this easy-to-make

quilt showcases bits of color and texture in a variety of shades.

It's a perfect contrast to the soft pastel colors of the storybook cottages,

and it will add delightful contrast to any spot in your home as well.

Materials

Yardage is based on 42"-wide fabric.

- 3¾ yards total of assorted white and cream fabrics for blocks and inner and outer borders
- 3¼ yards total of assorted green fabrics, ranging from light to dark green for blocks, inner border, and binding
- 4¾ yards of fabric for backing
- 80" x 80" square of batting

Choosing Your Fabrics

Your greens can range from light spring green to deep green in a variety of prints and solids. For your white and cream fabrics, choose as many as possible, from pure white to tan prints. The variety and contrast in the colors will give your quilt that extra sparkle!

Cutting

All measurements include ¼"-wide seam allowances.

From the assorted white and cream fabrics, cut a *total* of:

7 strips, 4⅞" x 42"; crosscut into 54 squares, 4⅞" x 4⅞"

4 strips, 4½" x 42"; crosscut into 12 rectangles, 4½" x 12½"

8 strips, 2½" x 42"

37 strips, 2½" x 21"

From the assorted green fabrics, cut a *total* of:

7 strips, 4⅞" x 42"; crosscut into 54 squares, 4⅞" x 4⅞"

16 strips, 2¾" x 21"

37 strips, 2½" x 21"

Making the Blocks

1. Sew the assorted green and cream 2½" x 21" strips together in pairs to make 37 strip sets. Press toward the green strips. Cut each strip set into 8 segments, 2½" wide (296 total). You will use 290 segments and have 6 left over.

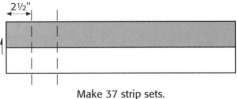

2½"

Make 37 strip sets.
Cut 8 segments from each strip set (296 total).

Cobblestones

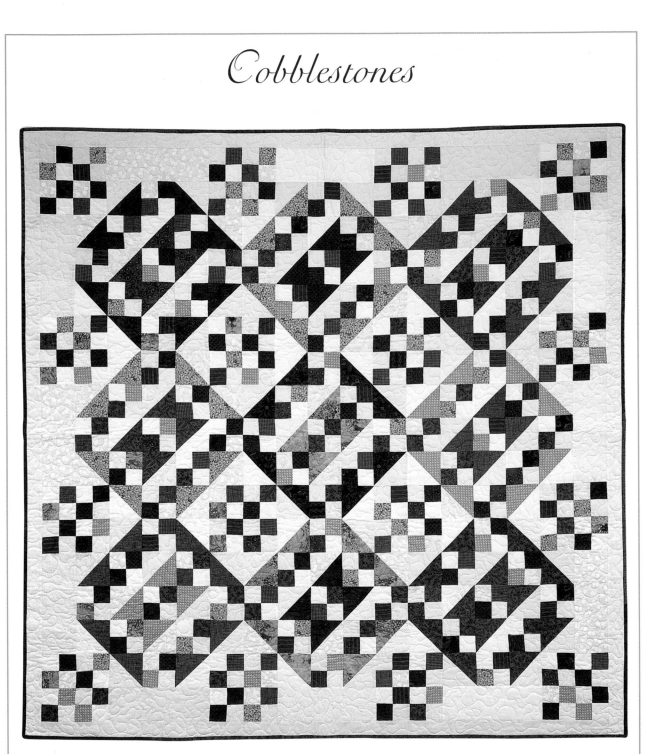

Finished quilt size: 72" x 72"

2. Sew the segments from step 1 into pairs as shown to make a total of 145 four-patch units for the blocks and border.

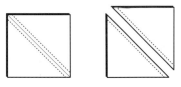

Make 145.

3. With a soft-lead pencil, draw a diagonal line from corner to corner on the wrong side of each of the assorted white or cream squares. Place each of the marked squares right sides together with one of the assorted green squares. Using your presser foot as a guide, stitch ¼" from both sides of the drawn line on each square. Cut along the drawn lines with scissors to make a total of 108 half-square-triangle units. Press the seams toward the green triangles.

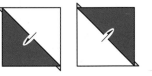

Make 108.

4. To make each block, arrange 13 four-patch units and 12 half-square-triangle units into five horizontal rows of five units each as shown. Stitch the units in each row together. Press the seams in alternate directions from row to row. The block should measure 20½" x 20½". Repeat to make a total of nine blocks.

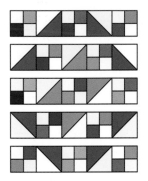

Make 9.

Assembling the Quilt Top

1. Referring to the quilt assembly diagram on the facing page, sew the blocks into three rows of three blocks each as shown. Sew the rows together. Press the seams in alternate directions from row to row.

2. To make the pieced inner border, arrange three assorted white or cream rectangles and six four-patch units from step 2 as shown. Stitch the pieces together. Press the seams toward the rectangles. Make 4.

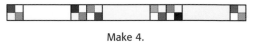

Make 4.

3. Refer to the quilt assembly diagram to stitch two of the inner border strips from step 5 to the quilt sides. Stitch one of the remaining four-patch units to the ends of the remaining inner border strips. Stitch the strips to the top and bottom edges of the quilt top.

4. Refer to "Adding Borders" on page 106 and the quilt assembly diagram to stitch the white and/or cream 2½" x 42" strips to the quilt top.

Finishing Your Quilt

Refer to "General Instructions," beginning on page 105, for specific instructions for each of the following finishing steps.

1. Layer the quilt top with batting and backing; baste.
2. Quilt in an allover pattern.
3. Sew the 16 assorted green 2¾" x 21" strips together end to end to make one long strip. Bind the quilt edges.

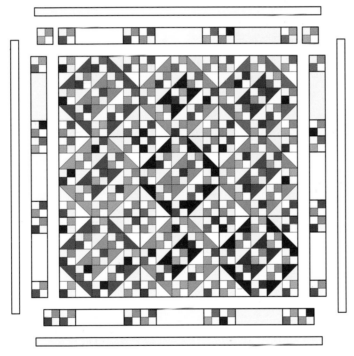

Quilt Assembly Diagram

Creating the Vintage Look

IN THIS VILLAGE of centuries-old cottages and cobblestone streets, a vintage-looking quilt is a perfect accent. The softened mellow shades of color reflect the ageless beauty and charm of the storybook surroundings.

Unfortunately, most of us aren't lucky enough to own such a quilted treasure, and even if we did, we probably would consider it far too precious to use in our homes. There is a wonderful way, however, to have a quilt with this timeless appeal and be able to enjoy using it, too. Make your own vintage-looking quilt!

Start with a scrappy design and keep it simple. In this quilt I've used light and dark four-patch scrappy blocks in rows that have been interspersed with an occasional 4½" square or half-square-triangle block. Yesterday's quilts were made from scraps that were available, and I wanted to re-create that look. Choose fabrics that have not been prewashed so that you will get maximum shrinkage when you wash the quilt later.

Cut your backing several inches larger than the quilt top and stretch it on a tabletop or other flat surface. This stretching is an important part of re-creating the vintage look, so take time to tape down all the edges as you stretch the backing. Next, layer thin cotton batting on top of the backing. Position the quilt top, right side up, on the batting and baste the layers together with plenty of pins. Machine quilt in the ditch between the blocks and through the center of larger blocks, making a 2" quilted grid. Add binding to the quilt.

And now for the important step: dyeing and shrinking your vintage-looking treasure. Wash the quilt in hot water, adding tan-colored, all-purpose dye to the water according to the manufacturer's instructions. Dry the quilt completely in the dryer on a high heat setting. The heat and agitation of washing and drying will give your quilt that well-used and well-loved vintage look.

Enjoy using your "almost antique" treasure!

General Instructions

This chapter includes helpful instructions for completing the projects in this book. You may instead use your own favorite techniques. To make sure you are pleased with your finished quilt, always keep in mind this basic but very important tip: Stitch accurate ¼"-wide seam allowances and press after each step before going on to the next one.

Freezer-Paper Appliqué

I used freezer-paper appliqué for the projects in this book; however, you may instead use your favorite type of appliqué, such as needle-turn, quick-fuse, or blanket-stitch appliqué.

1. Trace the appliqué patterns in reverse on the unwaxed (dull) side of the freezer paper. Cut out the templates on the traced lines.
2. Place the freezer-paper template, shiny side down, on the wrong side of the chosen fabric and pin it in place. Leave at least ¾" of space between pieces when attaching more than one freezer-paper template to the same fabric.
3. Cut out each shape, adding a ¼" seam allowance beyond the template edges.
4. Turn the allowance over the freezer-paper edge and press in place with the tip of a dry iron.
5. Place the appliqué on the background fabric and sew in place with an appliqué stitch (see "Hand Appliqué Stitch" at right).

6. On the wrong side of the appliqué shape, cut away the background fabric, leaving a ¼" seam allowance all around. Remove the freezer paper, using your fingers, a needle, or tweezers to gently pull it away from the appliqué.

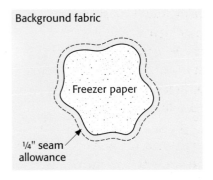

Hand Appliqué Stitch

Choose a long, thin needle, such as a Sharp, for stitching.

1. Tie a knot in a single strand of thread that closely matches the appliqué color.

2. Inserting the needle from the wrong side of the appliqué, bring the needle up on the fold line, and blindstitch along the folded edge. Take a stitch about every 1/8".

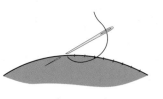

Appliqué Stitch

3. To end your stitching, pull the needle through to the wrong side. Take two small stitches, making knots by taking your needle through the loops.

Cutting Bias Strips

Bias strips, rather than strips cut on the straight grain of the fabric, are necessary whenever you are dealing with curves or curved edges. Use them when you cut fabric to make bias tubes for appliqué or when you cut strips for bias binding.

To cut bias strips, align the 45° angle marking of your rotary ruler with the selvage edge of a single layer of fabric that has been placed on your rotary-cutting mat. Cut as many bias strips as you need for your binding or bias tubes.

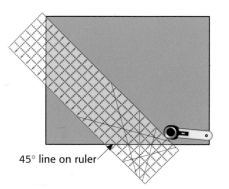

45° line on ruler

Adding Borders

Following are basic instructions for adding straight-cut borders to your quilt. Slight variations may occur throughout the book, depending on the borders for each project.

1. Measure the length of the quilt top through the center. Cut border strips to this measurement, piecing as necessary. Mark the center of the quilt-top sides and the border strips. Pin the border strips to the sides of the quilt top, matching the center marks and ends and easing as necessary. Sew the border strips in place. Press the seams toward the border.

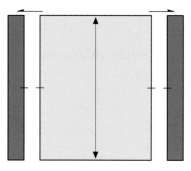

Measure center of quilt, top to bottom. Mark centers.

2. Measure the width of the quilt top through the center, including the side border strips just added. Cut border strips to this measurement, piecing as necessary. Mark the center of the quilt-top top and bottom edges and the border strips. Stitch the strips to the top and bottom edges of the quilt

top in the same manner as for the side border. Press the seams toward the border.

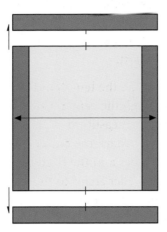

Measure center of quilt, side to side, including borders. Mark centers.

Layering the Quilt

The quilt "sandwich" consists of the backing, batting, and quilt top. I recommend cutting the quilt backing at least 4" larger than the quilt top on all sides. For large quilts, it is usually necessary to sew two or three lengths of fabric together to make a backing of the required size. Trim away the selvage edges (they are more difficult to quilt through) before sewing the lengths together. Press the backing seams open to make quilting easier.

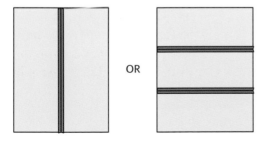

OR

1. Spread the backing, wrong side up, on a flat surface and anchor with pins or masking tape. Spread the batting over the backing, smoothing out any wrinkles.
2. Center the pressed quilt top, right side up, on top of the batting and smooth out any wrinkles. Make sure the edges of the quilt top are parallel to the edges of the backing.
3. All of the quilts in this book were machine quilted. For machine quilting, pin the layers together using #1 nickel-plated safety pins. Begin pinning in the center, working toward the outside edges and placing pins every 3" to 4" throughout.

Quilting

Choose your favorite quilting method to quilt your project. All of the projects in *English Cottage Quilts* were machine quilted by my very helpful long-arm quilter. Today many quilters enjoy the luxury of having their quilts finished by a talented professional quilter, and I'm among them! If you prefer to do your own machine quilting, check at your local quilt shop for books, stencils, or even classes to get you started.

Binding

If your quilt has curved edges, you must bind your quilt with bias-cut strips so that the binding curves smoothly around the edges. For straight edges, use the straight-cut binding technique.

Straight-Cut Binding

To make straight-cut, double layer (French) binding, I usually cut 2¾"-wide strips because I prefer a flat binding that doesn't look rounded on the edges. Cut binding strips across the fabric width. You will need enough strips to go around the perimeter of the quilt, plus about 10" for seams and the corners in the mitered folds.

1. With right sides together, sew the strips together on the diagonal as shown to create one long strip. Trim excess fabric and press the seams open.

2. Press the strip in half lengthwise, wrong sides together. Cut one end of the strip at a 45° angle and press it under ¼".

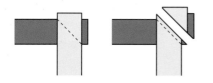

Fold line

3. Trim the batting and backing even with the quilt-top edges, making sure the corners are square.

4. Beginning on one edge of the quilt and using a ¼"-wide seam allowance, stitch the binding to the quilt, keeping the raw edges even with the quilt-top edge. End the stitching ¼" from the corner of the quilt and backstitch.

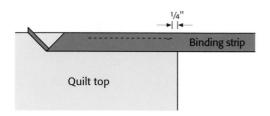

¼"

Binding strip

Quilt top

5. Fold the binding up, away from the quilt, then back down onto itself, aligning the raw edges with the quilt-top edge. Begin stitching at the edge, backstitching to secure, and end ¼" from the lower edge. Repeat the folding and stitching process on the remaining sides.

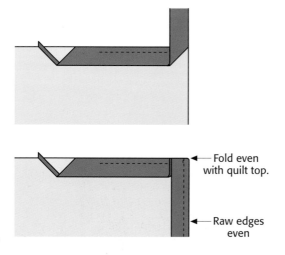

Fold even with quilt top.

Raw edges even

6. When you reach the beginning of the binding, lap the strip over the beginning stitches by about 1" and cut away any excess binding, trimming the end at a 45° angle. Tuck the end of the binding into the fold and complete the seam.

7. Fold the binding to the back of the quilt over the raw edges, with the folded edge just covering the machine stitching. Blindstitch in place, including the miter that forms at each corner.

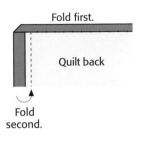

Fold first.

Quilt back

Fold second.

Bias Binding

Refer to "Cutting Bias Strips" on page 106 to cut enough bias strips to go around the perimeter of the quilt, plus about 10" for seams and any mitered folds. The project instructions will specify the width to cut the strips.

1. Follow steps 1–3 under "Straight-Cut Binding" on page 108 to assemble the bias strips and prepare the quilt for binding.
2. For rounded corners, begin adding the binding as directed in step 4 of "Straight-Cut Binding." Pin the binding around the first curve, taking care not to stretch the binding. Continue in this manner around the entire quilt and finish the binding as directed in steps 6 and 7.
3. For scalloped edges, as in "A Proper Garden" on page 50, gently stretch the bias binding around the inside curves as you machine stitch it to the quilt front. Fold the binding to the back, easing in fullness at the inside curves as you hand stitch.

About the Author

PAMELA MOSTEK BELIEVES that beautiful places inspire beautiful quilts. She used this artist's approach to design the quilts for her fourth book, *English Cottage Quilts*.

With her background and degree in art, she has experimented in a wide variety of areas, such as watercolor and decorative painting, weaving, and fabric surface design. About fifteen years ago she discovered the art of quilting, and it has been her passion ever since.

Pam loves working in various aspects of the quilting industry and spends her time writing and creating quilts for books and for her pattern company, Making Lemonade Designs, as well as designing fabric. A proud mother and grandmother, Pam lives with her husband in Cheney, Washington.

new and bestselling titles from

America's Best-Loved Craft & Hobby Books®

America's Best-Loved Quilt Books®

NEW RELEASES
20 Decorated Baskets
Asian Elegance
Batiks and Beyond
Classic Knitted Vests
Clever Quilts Encore
Crocheted Socks!
Four Seasons of Quilts
Happy Endings
Judy Murrah's Jacket Jackpot
Knits for Children and Their Teddies
Loving Stitches
Meadowbrook Quilts
Once More around the Block
Pairing Up
Patchwork Memories
Pretty and Posh
Professional Machine Quilting
Purely Primitive
Shadow Appliqué
Snowflake Follies
Style at Large
Trashformations
World of Quilts, A

APPLIQUÉ
Appliquilt in the Cabin
Artful Album Quilts
Blossoms in Winter
Color-Blend Appliqué
Garden Party
Sunbonnet Sue All through the Year

HOLIDAY QUILTS & CRAFTS
Christmas Cats and Dogs
Christmas Delights
Creepy Crafty Halloween
Handcrafted Christmas, A
Hocus Pocus!
Make Room for Christmas Quilts
Snowman's Family Album Quilt, A
Welcome to the North Pole

LEARNING TO QUILT
101 Fabulous Rotary-Cut Quilts
Casual Quilter, The
Fat Quarter Quilts
More Fat Quarter Quilts
Quick Watercolor Quilts
Quilts from Aunt Amy
Simple Joys of Quilting, The
Your First Quilt Book (or it should be!)

PAPER PIECING
40 Bright and Bold Paper-Pieced Blocks
50 Fabulous Paper-Pieced Stars
Down in the Valley
Easy Machine Paper Piecing
For the Birds
It's Raining Cats and Dogs
Papers for Foundation Piecing
Quilter's Ark, A
Show Me How to Paper Piece
Traditional Quilts to Paper Piece

QUILTS FOR BABIES & CHILDREN
Easy Paper-Pieced Baby Quilts
Even More Quilts for Baby
More Quilts for Baby
Play Quilts
Quilts for Baby
Sweet and Simple Baby Quilts

ROTARY CUTTING/SPEED PIECING
101 Fabulous Rotary-Cut Quilts
365 Quilt Blocks a Year Perpetual Calendar
1000 Great Quilt Blocks
Around the Block Again
Around the Block with Judy Hopkins
Cutting Corners
Log Cabin Fever
Pairing Up
Strips and Strings
Triangle-Free Quilts
Triangle Tricks

SCRAP QUILTS
Nickel Quilts
Rich Traditions
Scrap Frenzy
Spectacular Scraps
Successful Scrap Quilts

TOPICS IN QUILTMAKING
Americana Quilts
Bed and Breakfast Quilts
Bright Quilts from Down Under
Creative Machine Stitching
Everyday Embellishments
Fabulous Quilts from Favorite Patterns
Folk Art Friends
Handprint Quilts
Just Can't Cut It!
Quilter's Home: Winter, The
Split-Diamond Dazzlers
Time to Quilt

CRAFTS
300 Papermaking Recipes
ABCs of Making Teddy Bears, The
Blissful Bath, The
Creating with Paint
Handcrafted Frames
Handcrafted Garden Accents
Painted Whimsies
Pretty and Posh
Sassy Cats
Stamp in Color

KNITTING & CROCHET
365 Knitting Stitches a Year
   Perpetual Calendar
Basically Brilliant Knits
Crochet for Tots
Crocheted Aran Sweaters
Knitted Sweaters for Every Season
Knitted Throws and More
Knitter's Template, A
Knitting with Novelty Yarns
More Paintbox Knits
Simply Beautiful Sweaters for Men
Today's Crochet
Too Cute! Cotton Knits for Toddlers
Treasury of Rowan Knits, A
Ultimate Knitter's Guide, The

Our books are available at bookstores and your favorite craft, fabric, and yarn retailers. If you don't see the title you're looking for, visit us at **www.martingale-pub.com** or contact us at:

1-800-426-3126

International: 1-425-483-3313 • Fax: 1-425-486-7596 • Email: info@martingale-pub.com

For more information and a full list of our titles, visit our Web site.

8/03/Q